The Last Revolution

The Last Revolution

The Destiny of Over- and Underdeveloped Nations

BY **L.-J. Lebret**

Translated by JOHN HORGAN

With a Preface by
Rt. Rev. Msgr. GEORGE G. HIGGINS
Director, Department of Social Action
National Catholic Welfare Conference

SHEED AND WARD : NEW YORK

Preface

The Last Revolution is a very disturbing but also, on the whole, a very hopeful book. Its purpose is "to focus on essentials"—the essential causes of and remedies for the economic, social, and cultural misery which plagues the so-called underdeveloped countries and poses such an ominous threat to the security and peace of all mankind. Père Lebret is frank to admit that the preparation of the book has profoundly affected him. Reflecting on what he has seen and read about the extent of human misery in the world, he sees mankind "staggering in confusion from crisis to crisis, unable to solve problems which they avoid defining, not so much from intellectual incapacity as a willful refusal to question established but fallacious values."

American readers are warned in advance that Père Lebret, who is no respecter of persons or of nations, is disconcertingly impartial in his criticism of the "established but fallacious values" of the East and the West or, more specifically, of the Soviet Union and the United States. Indeed, if anything, he is more critical of the United States than of Russia, presumably because he expects a higher standard of performance from a nation which claims to be the showplace of democracy. "There are many reasons," he says, "for the reluctance of the more advanced and consequently richer peoples to take an objective view of the world situation. The main reason is a certain kind of greed, that is, an immoderate love of possession. The former colonial powers were often steeped in this vice, and never succeeded in freeing themselves from it. But the new major powers are also possessed by the same vice in an even more virulent form."

Père Lebret's specific references to the United States are brutally frank. "Americans," he says, for example, "continue to express surprise when they discover that their interventions on behalf of the underdeveloped nations (which they consider to be benevolent and which indeed are partially so) breed a slight but noticeable amount of resentment everywhere. This is because they have created a new form of colonialism, as odious as the original colonialism and even less imbued with respect and love."

This particular indictment of the United States I can accept with equanimity, but I would want to enter at least a mild rejoinder when Père Lebret, stepping out of his professional role as an economist, proceeds to indict our entire national culture. "The puritanism which presided over the birth of the United States," he writes, "has been toned down little by little. In the public eye material success has taken the place of work as the fundamental value. Money has become the yardstick of everything. This has produced a situation where determined values are ascribed to the material and tangible aspects of civilization. Otherwise how can we explain the fact that many Americans are more concerned with the size and architectural solidity of their schools than with what is taught within their walls? How otherwise can we understand the numerous dangers to which television, as well as illustrated criminal adventure stories, expose children every day, all for profit? If there is a conflict between the norms of art, education or culture on the one hand, and the demands of material profit on the other, the latter almost invariably have an easy victory."

Père Lebret, who does not know the United States from first-hand experience, is entitled to this opinion, but I suspect that his fellow countryman, Jacques Maritain, who lived in this country for many years and came to know it very well indeed, would not completely agree with him.

Be that as it may, Americans owe it to themselves to read Père Lebret's urgent plea for a new civilization with a completely open mind. To be sure, he is severely—and, some would think, excessively—critical of our response or lack of response to the world situation, but his criticism, "though argued in strong terms, must not be understood," he assures us, "as being prompted by any feeling of ill-will towards the United States. Rather do we wish," he continues, "because of our affection for Americans and without minimizing their faults, to offer them this warning. Their universal potential for doing good, if it were objectively applied, would earn them the moral prestige and affectionate recognition that they have not been able to obtain up to now."

Let us hope and pray that this word to the wise from one who is himself a very wise and learned counsellor will be taken to heart by at least a saving remnant of open-minded and open-hearted Americans—and the sooner the better, for if Père Lebret has read the signs of the times correctly, we have little time to spare. I am pleased to recommend his book enthusiastically, with only a handful of minor reservations which may indeed be unconsciously chauvinistic but, hopefully, do not reflect the alleged tendency of the United States habitually to act "without taking into account either the real needs of the rest of humanity or the urgent necessity for revising its own fundamental economic and political concepts."

RT. REV. MSGR. GEORGE G. HIGGINS
Director, Department of Social Action
National Catholic Welfare Conference

Contents

The Last Revolution

Introduction

The future of the world is not governed
by blind destiny; it has been placed
under our control. We have the power
to study and consider the facts and
translate our ideals into action.
                    —Gunnar Myrdal

The purpose of this book is to focus attention on essentials.
I should not have had the temerity to publish this work were
it not the fruit of personal observations made all over the
world. In some countries, such as Brazil, Colombia, Vietnam,
and Senegal, these observations took the form of detailed
and systematic studies; in other countries of Latin America,
Africa and Asia, comparisons are based on more cursory
impressions.

The preparation and compilation of this book have profoundly affected me. The evidence supplied by my own eyes
was even more strongly confirmed by an intensive study of
the reports and analyses which are now available to all.
Reflecting on what I had seen and read, I seemed to see
mankind staggering in confusion from crisis to crisis, unable
to solve problems which they avoid defining, not so much

from intellectual incapacity as a willful refusal to question established but fallacious values.

Neither the East nor the West will risk abandoning their "orthodox" positions, to which however their everyday behavior fails to conform. Fear of losing face is not confined to the Far East. Americans continue to proclaim themselves liberty-lovers and to criticize the colonial powers when they impugn the sovereignty of free nations; and the American economy so predominates that the non-Communist world is forced to follow its capricious lead. The Soviets, on the other hand, declare their Marxist principles while obviously misinterpreting or largely abandoning them in practice.

However I do not intend in this book to join in the battle between East and West, nor to make a choice between two intellectual and technical conceptions of world organization. The book is in no way directed against any man or any nation, and therefore I ask that the criticism offered here be accepted in the same spirit of charity in which it is made. My only hope is to make some of the people of the leading countries of East and West pause for thought, and to help them to realize that they cannot, without criminal folly, continue in outmoded attitudes which no longer correspond either to historical reality or to what the world expects of them.

The problem confronting the world is nothing less than the creation of a new civilization. There is a striking contrast between man's desire to prove his worth and his childish ideas of "going one better" than his neighbor, which he often confuses with being "better off." The rich are covetous, desiring more than they need; and this covetousness is rapidly spreading to the poorer peoples. A greedy world can only be a divided world, ethically sordid, heading towards barbarism. The West, in its exclusive self-preoccupation, is indeed on the verge of barbarism.

In order not to be accused of giving a merely subjective impression, I have not limited myself to my own personal observations. A single observer, no matter how honest he is, is always suspect. It is too easy to contradict his data and dismiss his deductions. For this reason I have relied mainly on documents published by the UN. Although statistics must be constantly updated, those used in this book are as valid today as when they were first taken.

Basing my findings in this way on official statistics and the most competent authorities, I have tried to show that my concern is not just an isolated phenomenon which can legitimately be discounted. My distressing journey through poverty and want has been lightened by the discovery that my own awakening to the situation is shared by many travelling on similar paths.

No *a priori* position inspired my action. It was with an honest love of humanity that I set myself to observe the facts and study the most reliable documents. Far from causing me to despair, the result of this patient research has convinced me that mankind, in spite of the heavy shackles of prejudice and tradition, is seeking a world-wide and brotherly solution. After all, it needs only a few steps forward on the part of one side and the other to arrive at this conclusion. I feel it my urgent duty to help towards this advance.

I believe that the world has now reached a stage when the only realistic answer is a Utopian one, a Utopia in which West and East look anew at the dogmas which envenom their actions, in order to make coexistence less full of fear, and to render possible constructive cooperation on the level which the needs of the times demand. The days of small-scale and ineffective adjustments are over.

Finally I need hardly say that in using the terms "advanced" and "underdeveloped" countries, I am speaking strictly from a technical and economic point of view, and am not making any comparison between differing cultures.

The Situation in the World Today

*The confused ideas at present held by
ill-informed men must be replaced
by a clear perception of a whole set of
serious problems.*

Part One

The Situation in the World Today:
ESSENTIAL DATA

1

An Unforeseen Increase in Population

Every year the world's population increases by
more than the total population of France.

THE IMPORTANCE OF THIS GROWTH

In the past population growth was slow and occasionally
even interrupted by decline. But during the last three centuries mankind has speeded up the rhythm of its growth.
The total world population is estimated to have increased
from less than 600 million in 1650 to some 2,400 million in
1950. The figures generally agreed on are 900 million in
1800, 1,150 million in 1850, and 1,600 million in 1900. In
other words, the world's population more than doubled itself
between 1650 and 1850, and again between 1850 and 1950.
It is also recognized that Europe, including the Russian
territories in Asia, had a five-fold increase in population
between 1650 and 1950.

Europe showed a rapid rise between 1850 and 1880;
growth then slowed down. However, some countries in
Western Europe showed an increase in their birth rate after
the Second World War.

Asia has more or less followed the world pattern. Its

population had grown from some 400 million in 1650 to about 1,300 million in 1950. The population of Africa, whose rate of growth remained static for several centuries, has increased more and more rapidly since the middle of the nineteenth century. The two Americas have had an amazingly high rate of growth. It is almost impossible to estimate what their population was 200 years ago. From only a few million it grew to more than 350 million by 1950.

The estimated world population in 1961 was 3,069 million, distributed as follows:

1,721 million in Asia,
430 million in Europe,
422 million on the American continents,
261 million in Africa,
218 million in the U.S.S.R.,
17 million in Oceania.

Between 1950 and 1961 the annual growth rate was 1.8, which means that the world population increased by 560 million, that is, by about 70 times as many people as live in and around London or New York. The actual growth figures for the different areas, as far as can be deduced from the annual demographic survey carried out by the United Nations in 1961, are these:

337 million in Asia,
35 million in Europe,
93 million on the American continents,
54 million in Africa,
37 million in the U.S.S.R.,
4 million in Oceania.

Roland Pressat, envisaging the possibility of rapid growth

TABLE 1

Projected World Population
(*in millions*)

Year	Underdeveloped Countries	Other Countries	Total
1955	1,800	900	2,700
1980	2,900	1,020	3,920
2005	4,000	1,150	5,150
2055	5,400	1,490	6,890

culminating in Malthusianism, gave as his projections for the evolution of the world's population the figures in Table 1.[1]

Even supposing—and this has not yet been proved—that fertility lessens rapidly, demographic expansion will however continue to be considerable. It may, in fact, become even more rapid, as the annual average increase rate of world population has risen in the last few years (1.6 per cent for the period 1950–1957; 1.8 per cent for the period 1957–1961).

According to Michel Cépède, three successive phases can be discerned in the evolution of any population: *stability, rapid growth,* and *further stability.*

During the first phase, when the food available is deficient in vegetable calories, both quantitatively (in ordinary calories) and qualitatively (in proportion to calories of animal origin), figures for both births and deaths are high and remain more or less

[1] Roland Pressat in *Le Tiers Monde* (Paris: Presses Universitaires de France, 1956), pp. 200–201, 203. *Le Tiers Monde* is a publication of the Institut National d'Etudes Démographiques (I.N.E.D.).

equal. The balance of population therefore remains constant, or varies from the norm by very little in either direction.

During the second phase, when the quantity of the food available increases, the death rate will begin to decrease while the birth rate remains at its former level. In other words, the population will tend to increase rapidly.

Finally during the third phase, when the food available undergoes its ultimate and primarily qualitative improvement, by virtue of an increase in the proportion of animal products it contains, the birth rate decreases in its turn and once more equals, more or less, the death rate.

This hypothesis, supported by many observations, shows that if a new equilibrium is to be established between population and resources, the potentially dangerous second phase must be as short as possible. Too slow progress will be obvious from the number of deaths rather than from the number of births, and will end in disaster; rapid progress will lead, after what will undoubtedly be a violent but short period of expansion, to the necessary balance between population and resources and a higher standard of living for all.[2]

Without any doubt the improvement in nourishment plays an important part in the reduction of the death rate; but apparently the lessening in mortality in the underdeveloped countries is not primarily ascribable to the improvement in economic conditions. It is due, above all, to modern medicine, vaccination, antibiotics, the campaign against disease-bearing insects, education, and the provision of elementary hygienic equipment. Some population groups have been able to effect a reduction in their death rates in this way in spite

[2] Michel Cépède, "La Situation alimentaire," *La Revue Socialiste* (April, 1955).

of the deterioration of their economic and social condition.

Alfred Sauvy's explanation of this development is that during economic development in the past, medicine followed after economic progress, and was never in a position to precede it. This is no longer the case. Advanced medical techniques are being abruptly introduced into what is, in many cases, a medieval economy. An almost illiterate hospital orderly can now give certain vaccinations and injections. Airplanes spray DDT on marshy land where natives still use no tools except primitive hoes and live in dread of their witch-doctors. The dissemination of these technical improvements is moreover inexpensive. The cost of the anti-malaria campaign per inhabitant varies in different countries from as little as 4.5 cents (in Baluchistan) to a dollar (in British Guiana).

If one takes all these factors into account, it seems likely that even the minimum predictions for population growth will have been more than fulfilled by the year 2000.

On the other hand, it is not certain that the rate of increase in the developed countries corresponds to that of Europe's most Malthusian countries. The American population, in effect, increases by three million every year, and there will be no foreseeable decrease in this figure. And France's demographic recovery since the war is a well known fact.

Mankind therefore is faced with the most formidable economic—and consequently social, political and ethical—problem it has ever had to solve. The most astounding thing is not that the problem should exist, but that there should be so much indifference to it, not only among the unthinking public, but among responsible figures in national and international affairs.

MORE THAN HALF THE WORLD'S POPULATION LIVES IN ASIA

If the predicted global increase in population is so considerable, the increase in Asia is no less striking. More than half the human race lives there. Five huge countries—China, India, Japan, Pakistan, and Indonesia—between them account for almost half the world's population. The people in these countries spring from very old civilizations which are at the same time capable—as Japan's experience proves—of adapting themselves to modern techniques and rapid industrialization, while at the same time being ready to accept less lavish living conditions than those to which the West has become accustomed.

In spite of the destruction and loss of life occasioned by the war with Japan and the Communist revolution, the population of China continues to show a large yearly increase. In 1958 it was estimated that there were 670 or 680 million Chinese. The annual birth rate is on the order of 40 per 1,000. Alarmed by this expansion and by the economic and social modifications it has brought with it, the Chinese government has now taken certain eugenic measures.

Japan, during the last hundred years or so, has been technically transformed and its population has more than tripled. The expectation of life there is now 58 years. This is the highest figure for any Asian country. Even if the birth rate were reduced by the birth control policy during and since the Occupation (it fell from 33.7 in 1948 to about 17 in

1960), the death rate was reduced from 12 to 7 during the same period. Japan therefore continues to increase in population at a rate which is approximately the same as the world average.

It was estimated recently that India and Pakistan are among the countries which have a low population increase. In India, according to official statistics, the birth rate fell from 33.3 per 1,000 in 1938 to about 22.5 per 1,000 during the 1958–1961 period. At the same time the death rate fell from 24.7 to 11.1 (in 1960), and the infant mortality rate from 167 to 85. The annual increase was obviously about four million a year. The expectation of life in India is at the moment 33 years, the lowest in the world. If the economic situation improves with the increase in the area of cultivated and irrigated land, the successful termination of development projects, and new hygienic measures, the prolongation of life expectancy will further increase the rate of growth.

India and China taken together will, at the present rate of growth, continue to constitute 40 per cent of the human race; and their huge populations will, considered as absolute figures, become decisive factors. They will accept poverty even if they continue to be poor, and they will dominate the "Great Powers" who today claim the leadership of the world.

As these nations develop their considerable potential, there will have to be a rapid reappraisal of the relationship between economic and military strength. The passiveness we attribute to Asiatics can easily become aggressiveness as the example of Japan, Indonesia, Korea, Vietnam, India, Pakistan, and Syria have shown us. Asia's awakening is taking place swiftly before our eyes, completely modifying the balance of power and drawing its support from historical or untapped mystical sources of strength.[3]

[3] For more recent statistics on population growth throughout the world, see the study of Michel Cépède, François Houtart and Linus Grond, *Population and Food* (New York: Sheed and Ward, 1964), chaps. 1, 2.

2

The World Is Unequally Developed

The average density of the agricultural population varies according to the region from as little as 3 to as many as 450 people per square mile.

If we consider that portion of the earth's surface which is in some way utilized, the density table of agricultural population per square mile can be seen in Table 2.

TABLE 2

Density of Agricultural Population
(*per square mile*)

Country	ploughed land, fallow land and orchards	meadow and pasture land
Asia (excluding U.S.S.R.)	798	441
Antilles and Central America	339	75
Europe (excluding U.S.S.R.)	258	156
Africa	249	63
South America	228	42
Oceania	66	3
United States and Canada	45	18

19

But these average figures conceal enormous differences. Thus, with respect to the land in the first column, many parts of Tanganyika have an agricultural population whose density ranges from 1389 to 2085 per square mile.

When we examine the relative importance of cultivated land and the density of the rural population in each country separately, the contrast between the developed countries and the others is shattering. Egypt's case is, without any doubt, the most astounding. (See Table 3.)

TABLE 3

Percentage of Cultivated Land and Density of Rural Population

Country	Cultivated land as percentage of total area	Rural population per sq. mi. of cultivated land
Netherlands	68	546
United Kingdom	65	255
United States	39	54
Canada	7	48
Australia	2.4	39
India	46	714
Ceylon	42	1353
Mexico	5	492
Brazil	2.8	420
Egypt	2.5	1626

This record for density seems to be surpassed by that of the rice-growing deltas in the Far East. These areas are home for a highly concentrated population whose numbers occasionally surpass 4,500 people per square mile, as in the Yang Tse Kiang delta.

China has about 217,000,000 acres of cultivated land for 680 million inhabitants; the United States has approximately 365,000,000 acres of cultivated land for a population that is less than a third of that of China.

There are approximately 4 acres of cultivated land for every person in Oceania, Canada and the United States; 2 acres in the U.S.S.R.; 1.5 acres in Latin America; .5 acres to .7 acres in South and East Asia; 1 acre in the Near East. One acre per person is the world average.

The Indians of the Andes seldom own more than one acre per family, and this plot is usually situated on a steep slope that has been exposed to erosion for centuries. In China the average area of a farm, before the change-over to collectives, was 4 acres. In Holland, it is 14 acres; in Denmark 39.25 acres; in England 63.75 acres; and in the United States 158.75 acres.

In Africa, as in the Andean countries, the white population is often in an ultra-privileged position. This, according to Gourou, is the reason for the fact that in Kenya 3 million natives own 33,333 square miles, while the country's 21,000 whites have 13,333 square miles. In Southern Rhodesia, 1.5 million natives occupy 38,333 square miles, and 60,000 whites occupy 61,666 square miles.

It is true that there are vast areas throughout the world which have yet to be brought under cultivation. It is estimated that 25 per cent of the land in Latin America is cultivable; 5 per cent has actually been cultivated. In Costa Rica only a tenth of the potentially cultivable land has in fact been cultivated. At the same time these estimates should be treated with caution; the study of soil contours, climatic conditions, and risk from erosion has rarely been systematically or scientifically carried out, and the term "cultivable land" has still to be properly defined.

The difficulty is increased when it comes to estimating the world's capacity for supporting a certain total population. This depends, in effect, on the level of nourishment which can be considered the minimum.

Pearson and Harper, the most pessimistic authorities, allow for a minimum figure of 2,800 million, taking Asiatic standards of nourishment as the norm; taking European figures as a guide, this figure would fall to 2,100 million; in the light of North American standards, to as few as 900 million. Other estimates have put the figure as high as 13,300 million.

To be frank, it appears that even where the most reliable authorities are concerned, the bases for these estimates do not seem to be completely trustworthy. Colin Clark predicted in 1949 that by the year 2000 the world's population would have reached 3,500 million and that the consumption of food would be 2.75 times what it was in 1938. Making predictions as outspoken as these would seem to be somewhat foolhardy.

Technological progress must of course be taken into account, as must also the inertia, suspicion and ignorance often displayed by rural populations, and the deficiencies in agricultural policies.

The diversity of output is amazing when one compares agricultural production per day per inhabitant, and that per day per acre.

The Food and Agriculture Organization of the UN (FAO)

has calculated that the production per day per inhabitant
of vegetable calories was, between 1934 and 1938, 10,000
in North America, 2,750 in the Far East, and 14,250 in North
Western Europe.

Production per cultivated acre per day ranged from 2,500
in North America, to 5,500 in the Far East, and to 7,500 in
North Western Europe. But per day and per rural inhabitant
—that is, everyone who lives in the country whether he
takes part in cultivation or not—the figure for North America was 15,720, that for the Far East 1,300, and that for
North Western Europe 5,700.

The effects of technical progress on the output of various
types of production have become generally available since
the war in those countries which have evolved to the greatest
extent. The underdeveloped countries, however, have not
benefited to the same extent from this progress.

In order to take stock of the different positions in which
countries find themselves, it is interesting to compare two
countries which are as different from each other as they
could possibly be, although both are great cotton-producing
countries—the United States and Egypt.

According to the UN there is 10 times as much land available for cultivation in the United States, in proportion to
the total population, as in Egypt, and 40 times as much in
proportion to the agricultural population. Moreover, this
estimate does not take into account the large areas of
prairies, pasture, or other forms of potentially cultivable
land which abound in the United States, but which are
practically non-existent in Egypt.

The intense development of cultivable land in Egypt,
made possible by the presence of a large labor force and by

virtue of the rich quality of the soil, gives a greater yield per acre than in the United States, where farming is mechanized. Nevertheless, the yield from the land in Egypt, compared to the total area, would have to be multiplied by forty to give the same yield per person as in the United States. It can also be predicted that Egypt's mortality rate, which is relatively high at the moment but falling slowly, will be radically reduced in the near future through public hygiene measures, and also that, as there is no sign that the birth rate will decrease in the foreseeable future, the already closely-packed agricultural communities will become even more congested.

The number of acres per head of the total population amounts to 0.3 in Egypt and 3 in the United States. The corresponding figures for acres in relation to the agricultural population alone are .425 and 16.75 respectively.

Gourou, among others, has underlined the serious errors of judgment that can be made by people who talk of the rich quality of tropical soil or of the soil in such countries as are already available for development. Tropical soil is frequently extremely loose and crumbly, severely affected by erosion, often threatened by subsidence or salinity, and exposed to floods or drought.

Where semi-tropical land is in question, we already know the destruction effected, for instance, by the combination of drought and a locust swarm, such as occurred in Morocco in 1957. We are also aware of the major migratory movements of the Brazilians who were driven from the northeast of their country to the south by drought between 1950 and 1953.

It is equally obvious that traditional farming methods

involving primitive systems of crop rotation cannot be quickly improved without the risk of creating social disintegration and the rapid exhaustion of the soil.

Nothing but on-the-spot study of the different factors involved will do before predictions can be made with any degree of objectivity.

3

Inequality in Life Expectancy

Life expectancy at birth varies enormously depending on the degree of economic development in the country concerned. In some countries it is twice as high as in others. To compare life spans we usually examine three sets of figures: those for infant mortality, general mortality, and those for life expectation from birth.

THE REDUCTION OF INFANT MORTALITY

Infant mortality was formerly a considerable factor in every country in the world, and this was the main reason for the slow population increase. The accompanying table demonstrates the impressive speed with which the more developed countries have cut down the number of deaths occurring in the year after birth.

On the other hand, infant mortality in the North African countries still reaches a figure of between 150 and 200 per thousand, and in the Negro population in South Africa it reaches 200–300 per thousand. In addition, the age when children are particularly susceptible to disease is extended to cover considerably more than the first year of life, and it

TABLE 4

Infant Mortality Rate per Thousand Live Births

	1936	*1948*	*1957*
Sweden	43	23	15
United Kingdom	62	36	22
U.S.A.	57	32	25
Belgium	86	59	26
West Germany		58	32
France	67	56	26

is not unusual to find that epidemics have killed so many children that the infant mortality rate is as high as 500 per thousand.

The accompanying *approximate* figures give some idea of this in 1957.[1]

Cuba, Mexico, Paraguay	125
Bolivia, Brazil, Colombia, Ecuador, Honduras, Nicaragua, Panama, Peru, Dominican Republic, Venezuela	150
Guatemala, El Salvador, Thailand	175
India, Pakistan, Philippines	200
Burma	225

These figures seem to have dropped since 1957; *but some countries still have an infant mortality rate that is ten times as high as in the countries where it is lowest, such as Sweden, New Zealand, and the Netherlands.*

[1] UN, *Report on the World Social Situation* (February 27, 1957).

THE REDUCTION IN OVERALL
MORTALITY RATES

The overall mortality rate for the developed countries of Europe and for North America, for which reliable statistics are available, has now fallen to 10 per thousand. Figures for most of the underdeveloped countries are doubtful. While they may show an obvious reduction in the overall mortality rate, this must not be exaggerated, because of the complexity of the situation. Roland Pressat, in *Le Tiers Monde*, has warned us against this, quoting the example of India and Ceylon.

Apart from the Bombay famine in 1943, India experienced no serious famines between 1930 and 1945. It has also seen victory over formerly fatal diseases—the plague is a case in point. But because vaccinations have not been effected over a wide enough area and because the sick have not been properly isolated, cholera has not yet completely disappeared although its incidence is decreasing.

Ceylon, where organization has reached a higher pitch of efficiency, has been able to combat famine and most fatal diseases since 1925. But in the absence of appropriate methods, the anti-malaria struggle has had little success. In Ceylon never less than 20 per cent and sometimes as many as 50 or 60 per cent of the population succumbed regularly to the disease until 1947. Then the anti-malaria campaign was organized and thanks to this, the average life span in Ceylon rose from 42.8 years in 1946 to 59.8 in 1954. Finally, hygienic progress in the underdeveloped countries has enabled people to live for longer without materially affecting their standard of living.

LIFE EXPECTANCY AT BIRTH

Life expectancy at birth is the average life span of one generation which will die out at the present mortality rate of the population in a particular area.

This expectancy exceeds 68 years in the more fortunate countries (Germany, Austria, Belgium, France, Czechoslovakia, South Africa, and Canada), and approaches or exceeds 70 years in the most advanced countries (Norway, the United Kingdom, Sweden, Switzerland, Denmark, Finland, Holland, the United States, Australia, and New Zealand).

The difference between these and the underdeveloped countries is much more marked: Brazilians, Egyptians and Mexicans have a life expectancy of less than 50 years at birth. In India the figure is 33 years.

Two conclusions can be drawn from these figures. In the first place, to the degree that hygienic and medical precautions become more widespread, the numerical superiority of the people in the underdeveloped countries will become even more obvious. In the second place, as infant mortality is reduced and the average life span prolonged, the burden on the active percentage of the population will become greater. In underdeveloped areas, 55 workers support 40 young people and 5 aged ones—a much higher figure than that for the developed areas, where between 60 and 64 workers support between 36 and 40 unproductive people.

Assuming that everyone under 15 and over 65 is "dependent," it can be seen that in the developed European countries, 10 productive people support between 3 and 4.5

non-productive ones, and that the same number of workers in Asia, Africa and Latin America have to support as many as eight dependents.

This chapter can be summed up by referring to the reflections of the authors of the *Atlas géographique alimentaire*.

Undernourished people die before others. At birth they have a much shorter life expectancy . . . the racial factors cannot be taken into account since the population of the Mediterranean, Central America and Eastern Europe, who are almost exclusively white, have a higher mortality rate than the people of Western Europe, Australia, North America and even Argentina.

There is a striking similarity between the graph of food values and that of the overall mortality rates: countries which have the most and the best food, such as North America, Western Europe and Australasia, are also those where the mortality rate is lowest (and life expectancy at birth highest).[2]

[2] *Atlas de Géographie alimentaire* in *Documentation Française* (Paris, 1954), p. 34.

4

Inequality in the Face of Disease

People most prone to sickness are the poor,
because they are ill-equipped to combat the
spread of disease.

The inhabitants of the semi-tropical, tropical and equatorial zones are not only unprotected against diseases suffered in Western countries, but are also susceptible to numerous illnesses which are almost totally unknown, even by name, to the average European. These can be defined as "crowd illnesses." They are so widespread and affect such a high percentage of the population that they play a considerable part in hindering a country's economic and social development. They form a vast reservoir, as it were, of ill-health which must be dealt with before a country can have a reasonable chance of development.

ILLNESSES OF THE UNDERDEVELOPED COUNTRIES

Deficiency Diseases

These diseases are caused by undernourishment, that is to say a qualitative or quantitative deficiency in diet. They are the result of both poverty and ignorance.

Clinically they can be divided into beriberi, pellagra, scurvy, rickets, nutritional anaemia, and kwashiorkor. Kwashiorkor, for example, chiefly affects children between the ages of six months and six years. It is particularly evident among children who are subjected during the weaning period, and that immediately following it, to a diet which lacks animal protein. If the child survives, he remains particularly susceptible to cancer of the liver, and will probably live in a state of chronic deficiency.

Ignorance and taboos encourage the spread of deficiency diseases in countries where the food level, even if it is sufficiently rich in calories, is badly balanced, because every untimely change in a system all of whose other aspects remain unchanged, can have disastrous results.

Infectious Diseases

These diseases are extremely contagious and provoke widespread epidemics. The best known is bubonic plague, in all its forms. Originating in rats or other wild rodents, it is transmitted to man by fleas. This devastated China and Manchuria in 1910, with a death toll of 60,000. In some years the number of deaths from this frightening disease in India has exceeded 1 million. It is also prevalent in certain parts of Africa, such as South Africa and Madagascar, and in the Americas.

Cholera and yellow fever are on the wane, but there are still large areas in South America and in Africa where yellow fever is endemic.

Smallpox can, in its most serious manifestations, account for a death rate of 30 per 100 or, in its milder forms, of less than 1 per 100. It is still prevalent, particularly in Africa,

South America, Asia and India, where its most serious out-breaks occur.

Typhoid is transmitted through lice. It is endemic in Egypt, Eritrea and Ethiopia; lesser epidemics occur in the entire area stretching from the Sudan through Uganda to Basutoland. Recurrent fever, also transmitted by lice, often accompanies typhoid epidemics.

Debilitating Diseases

These weaken the human frame to the point where all normal work becomes impossible. Leprosy, above all, ravages Western Africa where it incapacitates more than 200,000 of the 17 million inhabitants.

Malaria is a particularly severe scourge of humanity. It is endemic in the humid tropical zones; and before the inception of the anti-malaria campaign, it was a chronic problem in such Mediterranean countries as Italy, Greece and Cyprus, in the Southern states of the U.S.A., and else-where as well. It is present in its most severe forms in the underdeveloped countries where the population is very con-gested; in Bengal, for example, more than half the entire population succumbs to it from time to time. It has been said that 3 million people die from malaria every year. This estimate may be exaggerated, but at least it shows how widespread is the disease.

The mortality rate from tuberculosis is quite probably even higher than that from malaria. TB is more widespread, geographically speaking, than malaria; it probably affects every country in the world. And it is not confined to the underdeveloped countries. In fact, urbanization and in-dustrialization are two factors which combined most encourage the spread of the disease. It is probable that TB, as opposed to malaria, was not originally very prevalent among African tribes, but the conditions of modern living, notably in the townships, in conjunction with industrialization, have increased the risk of infection and facilitated the spread of the disease. The development of that continent and the changes wrought in the living habits of its population—particularly the wholesale migration of working populations and the establishment of roads and railways between Africa's different regions—have greatly encouraged the dissemination of this disease to which, until now, Africans have acquired only a very slight immunity.

Syphilis is also a world-wide disease. No sooner is it introduced into any relatively primitive group of people than it grows to enormous proportions. In the Ghund valley of India, for instance, clinical examinations revealed that 65 per cent of the entire population were affected.

Syphilis and framboesia (yaws) are similar in many respects, but are now considered as two different diseases. There are no exact figures of their incidence in the under-developed countries; but it can safely be said that they are widespread and are particularly prevalent where population is heavily congested.

Yaws was an ever-present disease in the Antilles, India, Malaysia, and in the Pacific islands as well as throughout Africa's tropical regions. It normally appears only on low-lying ground, and it is estimated that in the course of various campaigns carried out to eradicate it in Haiti, Indonesia, Iraq and Thailand, 300,000 people were treated. The results of these campaigns in Southeast Asia and the West Pacific are impressive. In 1963 about 80 out of the 135 millions living in these regions, where the disease is endemic, were completely freed from this scourge.

The UN's *Report on the World Social Situation* of 1957 adds to an already long list ankylostomiasis, bilharziosis, sleeping sickness, filariasis, trachoma, dysentery, typhoid fever and so on. Before leaving this subject, it should be noted that, especially where the aboriginal population of Latin America is concerned, there are two major factors leading to ill-health: the consumption of alcohol and of coca.

As Peruvian experts have now commented, the South American Indians have the choice of three "escape routes": migration, when they cannot find any cultivable land in their own village; coca, to mask their hunger pangs; and alcohol, to alleviate their misery. It is estimated that between 30 and 50 per cent of the adult population has recourse to coca, in the regions where it is available, but that the proportion rises to as high as 90 per cent in the case of miners who have to work far underground. Coca reduces the feeling of hunger and gives a momentary enthusiasm for the work at hand, but this is quickly replaced by the original feeling of apathy.

It is scandalous that, in some regions, alcohol and coca form part of the payment in kind given to the workers.

THE WORLD HEALTH CAMPAIGN AND ITS SHORTCOMINGS

The Campaign

There is one comforting aspect of this dramatic picture. Campaigns against disease have already gone into operation on a world-wide basis. Thanks to modern methods such as vaccination, DDT, antibiotics and the sulfa drugs, some diseases have practically been eradicated.

In Ceylon the anti-malaria campaign, which was instituted in 1946 and has been systematically carried out since then at the moderate expense of 24.5 cents per inhabitant, has reduced the number of malaria cases from 413 to 13 per 1,000 inhabitants. It is estimated that in Venezuela more than 2 million people were protected from the disease in 1952. The mortality rate from malaria, which was 173 for every 100,000 inhabitants in 1945, fell to 2 per 100,000 by 1952. Almost half the population of Southeast Asia (estimated at 250 million) has been included in the campaign to wipe out this scourge.

In Japan the campaign against TB has reduced the mortality rate from this disease from 1.87 per 1,000 inhabitants in 1947 to as few as 0.82 in 1952.

In Mexico, which was severely afflicted by smallpox in the past, the continual efforts to combat it since 1942 have produced such an improvement that no deaths from malaria were registered in 1952.

Swamp fever, too, has been almost completely eliminated from Brazil by DDT.

The English-sponsored campaign against diptheria in different parts of the world has achieved a reduction from 50,000 annual cases in 1941 to 600 in 1951.

The Shortcomings of the Campaign

In spite of these striking results tremendous efforts still have to be made to improve the organization of sanitary measures in the underdeveloped countries, where hunger and illness prevail. This situation demands resources and technical know-how which the majority of these nations simply do not possess.

Some statistics will help to give one an idea of the size of the problem.*

	Population per doctor	*Population per hospital bed*
Far East:		
Indonesia	71,000	1,300
Vietnam	22,000	2,500
Pakistan	15,000	
Malaysia	7,300	205
Africa:		
Nigeria	35,000	2,200
Cameroons	30,000	
Niger	96,000	
Egypt	2,800	600
Latin America:		
Guatemala	6,300	
Brazil	2,500	310
Argentina	760	160
More advanced countries:		
United Kingdom	1,200	85
Japan	940	196
France	930	65
Canada	930	77
U.S.A.	790	101
U.S.S.R.	550	155

* Statistics taken from the World Health Organization *Chronicle* (1962), no. 3.

The gap, obviously, is enormous. There are between 550 (U.S.S.R.) and 96,000 (Niger) people for every doctor, and between 65 (France) and 2,500 (Vietnam) for every hospital bed—without taking into account any possible discrepancy between the competence displayed by various doctors and the quality of the equipment in various hospitals.

Even the discouraging figures for the number of people to every doctor can give too optimistic an impression of the actual strength of the medical personnel available. It is clear that qualified doctors—and this is frequently the case in the underdeveloped countries—tend to set up their practices in the cities and heavily populated areas, neglecting the villages and the rural settlements.

THE CONSEQUENCES

If a man is to be fully productive, he must be in good health. This fact has been ignored far too often. Together with the United Nations experts, we must here insist on its importance.

A labor force that is in good health, confident and sure of itself, is just as important as hydroelectric stations, irrigation projects, and the discoveries being made in modern metallurgy and chemistry.

This aspect of the problem of development occurs again and again in reports prepared by the United Nations or its specialist agencies, which draw particular attention to the twin factors of malaria and malnutrition. It is estimated that malaria affects 300 million people every year, and that every person so affected loses between 20 and 40 working days. An inquiry carried out in the Philippines in 1946 revealed that malaria accounted for between 40 and 50 per cent of the absenteeism among primary and secondary school pupils. In the light of these figures it is not hard to estimate roughly how great a proportion of the adult population is affected in the same way. But many other debilitating diseases too affect hundreds of millions of people by reducing their capacity for work, for adaptation and for creativity.

According to one international expert, if the active life of the average Latin American were prolonged by 5 years, if the overall mortality rate were reduced by 5 per 1,000, and if absenteeism were reduced by 20 per cent (goals which are by no means out of reach), at least 10 million dollars would be saved every year in Latin America, taking the annual average value of one man's work as 500 dollars.

Even if we admit that this evaluation of the Latin American worker is three times higher than it is in practice, this hypothesis would still give Latin America a very real opportunity of establishing the economic substructure it so urgently needs.

Abel Wolman has given us a historical example of the importance of good health, taking the Panama Canal as his exemplar. Here the French, in spite of their enthusiasm, their technical knowledge, the high quality of their provisions, living quarters and even technical equipment, were completely defeated. The Americans succeeded, by the expedient of allotting 5 per cent of the total budget for the project to a campaign to eliminate the plague of mosquitoes and make the area in which they were working more healthy.

The underdeveloped peoples, unfortunately, are seldom in a position to take similar precautions.

Deficiency diseases, contagious diseases, and those transmitted by parasites, all sap man's capacity for hard, prolonged effort. Concealed forms of unemployment are often blamed for the low productivity, but this sort of unemployment is often in direct relation to the state of the worker's health. It reduces an already weakened man to the point where he is no longer able to work except in an intermittent manner, or even becomes a complete burden on his family group.

The elimination of one disease has the same implications as the discovery of a new country or a journey to a new frontier. This is amply demonstrated by the Indian state of Uttan Pradesh in the Himalayan Terai, where more than 1,250,000 acres of fertile land had been swallowed up by the jungle over 1,000 years ago, because swamp fever had killed or driven out those who tilled the land. Now, after an intensive anti-fever campaign, the jungle has been driven back and people are living on the land again.

5

The Unequal Struggle Against Hunger

Nearly half the human race is constantly hungry, and this state of affairs instead of improving is becoming more serious every day.

THE NUTRITIONAL LEVEL IS TOO LOW

The Need for Calories

It is generally admitted that people living in temperate climates require at least 2,700 calories a day. For manual laborers, this figure rises to 4,500 calories. A slightly lower level is acceptable in tropical climates, provided it is realized that this will be accompanied by a slight reduction in productivity.

Generally speaking, people in the developed countries consume between 2,750 and 3,250 calories every day, and this figure remains constant.

The accompanying table shows the inequality that exists between different countries, and this inequality is even more marked than appears at first. This is because agricultural produce, when it is used to feed animals, loses the greater part of its calorific value before it reappears as milk, fat or meat. International research organizations admit that for every calory contained in meat or milk, 7 vegetable calories have been consumed by the animal in question.

Average Consumption per Person per Day*

	Calories	Total Protein (grams)	Animal Protein (grams)
Far East:			
India (1960–61)	1,990	53	6
Pakistan (1959–60)	2,080	48	7
Philippines (1960)	1,950	49	15
Near East:			
United Arab Republic			
(1958–59)	2,520	73	12
Turkey (1959–60)	2,830	91	16
Latin America:			
Argentina (1959)	2,950	91	48
Brazil (1957)	2,650	67	19
Mexico (1957–59)	2,440	68	20
Peru (1959)	2,060	52	13
Africa:			
Libya (1959)	2,180	53	10
South Africa (1959–60)	2,570	74	32
More Advanced Countries:			
France (1959–60)	2,990	99	53
United Kingdom (1960–61)	3,270	87	52
New Zealand (1960)	3,490	110	75
U.S.A. (1960)	3,120	92	65

* No recent reliable statistics are available for Communist China, North Africa, etc. As to the weight criterion used in this table, a gram is roughly 35 percent, or slightly more than one-third, of an ounce.

For greater convenience, we describe the sum of the calories effectively consumed by the individual, as well as those lost when feeding animals in order to produce foodstuffs of animal origin, as "vegetable calories."

We can now take another example and compare the case of the Cingalese and that of the New Zealanders in this respect. In terms of net calory intake, the latter consume almost twice as much as the Cingalese; but in fact they consume a great deal more, because 51 per cent of the New Zealander's calories are of animal origin. In Ceylon the proportion of calories of animal origin is as low as 4 per cent. Rapid calculation will show that New Zealanders consume 5 times as many vegetable calories as the Cingalese. *People with a high standard of living eat five times as much per person as those at the other end of the scale.*

The gap is therefore extremely wide, and one-third of the world's population, in fact, consume less than the absolute minimum of calories. This dietary inequality, however, is not only quantitative. Sufficient nourishment presupposes the consumption of protective food such as animal protein, mineral salts, and vitamins. These are not to be found in the diet of a quarter of the number of people living below or near the minimum calorific level. This considerable nutritional deficiency prevents most forms of normal human activity. The need for calories, therefore, is only one of the nutritional shortages affecting mankind.

The Need for Proteins

Josué de Castro has shown the important position occupied by proteins in the dietary framework:

One of the most serious and widespread forms of deficiency—of specific hunger—is the lack of proteins. Protein forms the essential elements in the structure of living protoplasm and represents therefore the foundation of life itself. It is a very complex chemical substance which plants produce by utilizing the nitrogen from the soil, carbon from the air and other elements from the atmosphere, combining them all with the energy-producing action of sunlight. Only plants are capable of this miracle of creation. Animals, though they lead a far more active life, do not possess the magical capacity to produce living matter from an amalgam of inorganic elements. In this respect, humans and the other animals always depend on the vegetable world for their existence. In spite of the fact that he exists almost everywhere, man can exist only wherever he can find a vegetable basis for his existence. In the final analysis, man must always be a vegetarian either directly, by utilizing vegetable foodstuffs, or indirectly by eating the flesh of animals which themselves owe their existence to the vegetable world.[1]

The second column in the table just cited shows the average consumption of protein in grams per person per day. Here the difference between the developed and underdeveloped countries is 1 to 2. This inequality, too, may seem relatively slight. But in fact the proportions of animal protein in the total make it quite clear that this inequality is very considerable. Only animal proteins are complete. They are biologically more valuable than vegetable proteins since they contain the various amine acids that the human organism needs. A shortage of complete proteins reduces the organ's resistance to disease, and especially to infectious diseases such as TB, pneumonia, dysentery and typhus. The importance of animal protein is clear from this. And from this point of view the difference is considerable: the French

[1] Josué de Castro, *Geography of Hunger* (Boston: Little, 1952).

eat 8 times as much meat as the Indians, the Americans 11 times as much.

In Alfred Sauvy's estimation the increasing consumption of meat among the richer or more leisured classes in an over-populated country is equivalent to the elimination of the weakest, taking calories lost in the feeding of livestock into account. When a relatively large proportion of the population becomes meat-eating, the optimal consumption diminishes. The weak are eliminated. In an over-populated country, "to eat meat is to eat men."

To the need of calories and of protein should be added that of calcium, for calcium deficiency causes rickets; and the need of other vitamins to ward off beriberi, scurvy, pellagra and eye diseases.

The significance of the table must be seriously weighed. It should be clear that it is an extremely important set of figures. But we should not forget something of primary importance, which is that these figures are only *average* ones; in other words, a large proportion of the people to whom they apply are clearly below this nutritional level. In effect, therefore, there is considerable social inequality in the majority of the underdeveloped countries. The existence of a small number of people who enjoy a relatively high standard of living increases the average figure, but heavily disguises the very real misery which afflicts almost the entire population. The population of Asia, Africa and a large part of Latin America suffers permanently from hunger. In the same way these figures represent only annual averages, and do not show whether there is any seasonal aggravation in the condition of those who go hungry. Some tribes in Black Africa for instance reach or even exceed a nutritional level of some

3,000 calories for a large part of the year, but suffer from famine for several weeks and sometimes even for months.

A GIGANTIC PROBLEM TO BE SOLVED

In one of its latest publications, *Agricultural Production —Estimates for the Year 1970,* FAO attempts to forecast the amount of food production and requirements in 1970. These forecasts are based on two different hypotheses with regard to the rate of increase in national incomes.

According to the first, more optimistic, hypothesis, the underdeveloped countries will still go hungry in 1970 owing to inequalities in income, but undernourishment will be much less widespread than it is today.

The second, pessimistic, hypothesis calculates that the increase in calories in the poorer countries will be barely more than half that estimated by the first forecast. Hunger will thus still be prevalent and will still represent an urgent problem.

In any case, even taking the first and more favorable hypothesis, the average ration of animal protein per person per day will advance only from 7 to 10 grams in the Far East (this does not include the mainland of China and Japan), whereas the present figure is 40 grams for the European Economic Community countries and 65 for the U.S.A.

Because the long-term tendency of agricultural production, taken over the last ten years and compared with the pre-war period, has been to outdistance the increase in population, the quantity of food per head has grown and will probably grow even more; but qualitatively the situation of the underprivileged peoples will be just as catastrophic as it is today.[2]

Consequently an immense effort has still to be undertaken to conquer world hunger which, to quote Lord Boyd, "is more dangerous than the atom bomb for the future of the human race."

Is it not amazing that such warnings have so little effect on the privileged sections of the world as a whole?

[2] For a detailed analysis of food production and distribution, see the remarks of Michel Cépède, François Houtart and Linus Grond in *Population and Food* (New York: Sheed and Ward, 1964), chaps. 6, 7.

Part Two

The Situation in the World Today:
MISERY'S VICIOUS CIRCLE

Men are poor because their productivity
is low and their productivity is low
because they are too poor to produce
more.

—P. Rycmans

"A European does four times the work of an Arab, and an Arab four times that of a Negro." This well-known statement contains no element of natural truth. Suitably nourished, the African worker can show exactly the same results as his fellow worker in the temperate zones.

At the same time, this much-repeated statement serves to underline one depressing fact. Unequal productivity is only a reflection of dietary inequality. In other words, misery breeds misery; and the penniless man, left to his own devices, does not have the means to put an end to his poverty.

Whole countries are afflicted by hunger. Lacking sufficient food resources to ensure an adequate nutritional level, they are prone to illness and disease. They cannot find in themselves the strength necessary to break through the vicious circle of their misery.

Gunnar Myrdal denounced this vicious circle—sickness, poverty, underproductivity, undernourishment—as long ago as 1952. "People are ill because they are poor; they become even poorer because they are ill, and accumulated poverty engenders, in its turn, more sickness."[*] This is a cumulative process which operates through the continual lowering of standards and in which one negative factor is both the cause and the effect of all the other negative factors.

The vicious circle will not be broken until the privileged nations, faced by the growing hunger in the underdeveloped countries, abandon their obsession about production surpluses for another, and far more realistic obsession about coordinated international development. If they do not realize that this is the most urgent and important task which humanity, working in concert, has to achieve, they will prepare the way for a harvest of discontent, misery and revolt.

Now that we have described how unequal nations are in terms of their essential needs, we must try to analyze their inequality in the light of the conditions which are necessary before development can become reality.

[*] Gunnar Myrdal, "Les Aspects économiques de la santé," *Revue Economique* (November, 1952), p. 787.

6

Obstacles to Agricultural Development

*The most undernourished people are also those
in whose countries agricultural production
is in a decline.*

The graph of world agricultural production shows that at
the moment it is slightly ahead of the world's total requirements of food. But the situation varies in different regions,
and we have already noted that the inequality between the
developed and underdeveloped countries is striking.

The graph of North America reveals that production out-
strips population growth by a considerable amount, while
the Far East still produces less food than in the pre-war
period. In Latin America agricultural production has increased, but it is still lagging behind the increase in population. Africa's production alone has increased by more than
the demographic factor.

If we compare present-day food production with that
between 1925 and 1929, the most prosperous between-war
period, we can see that agricultural production is falling
below, or remains only very slightly above the necessary
minimum in the countries which were underdeveloped at
that time, while such production in the advanced countries

51

shows a rapid increase, further emphasizing the gap which separates them from the poorer nations.

Among the measures which have to be taken to ensure a progressively better agricultural yield are intensive farming with the appropriate technical equipment; soil preservation; the use of fertilizers, and mechanization. This last factor presupposes the availability of capital investment funds for agriculture. But even in such a case precautions have to be taken against accelerating the exhaustion or deterioration of the soil.

SOIL EXHAUSTION AND THE LACK OF FERTILIZERS

In many parts of tropical Africa, soil exhaustion can be seen to be responsible for a decrease in productivity. The history of the last 50 years shows us why. The introduction of truck farming, population growth and, where Europeans were in control, a reduction in the amount of land at the disposition of the native tribes, all contributed to a reduction in the amount of fallow land and led to exhaustion of the soil. To these factors can be added erosion, deforestation, the excessive use of land for pasturage, and defective farming methods.

Of course a great deal of exhausted land can be reclaimed, particularly through the use of natural manure and chemical fertilizers. The use of natural manure, however, is a characteristic of a more highly evolved farming technique, and the use of chemical fertilizer is too difficult a burden for the peasant populations in the underdeveloped areas. Only the fully developed countries have enough fertilizer at their disposal. Europe alone uses more than half the chemical fertilizer available in the world as a whole.

In the retarded countries fertilizer must be used if agricultural production is to be intensified and full advantage taken of developing agrarian techniques. The first task is to establish in as many of the underdeveloped countries as possible an organization which will take soil samples to ascertain what kind of fertilizer, and how much of it, can be used to the greatest effect in any particular case. The rational application of fertilizer is the only way to increase the strength of the fertile elements in the soil and, consequently, the only way to institute the most productive agricultural system possible.

The known reserves of raw material can certainly provide us with a great deal more fertilizer. The chief obstacle in many areas is lack of the capital necessary to buy the raw material and erect the expensive factories needed to produce modern fertilizers. Governments and international organizations must act together to provide the necessary funds and raw materials. National as well as international organizations must undertake agronomic research to ensure the best possible use of the available resources, such as fertilizers. Their help is also needed to show farmers how to use fertilizer in a rational way. The necessity of shaping some kind of a price policy must also be considered, and so must the desirability of making special credit terms available in order to back up such an ambitious campaign.

The underdeveloped countries at the moment are far from being able to call upon sufficient resources of fertilizer to ensure both the important increase in their production and the preservation, if not the improvement, of their lands.

THE LOW DEGREE OF MECHANIZATION

Where the transition to mechanized farming is concerned, the same backwardness can be observed in the underdeveloped countries. In addition, if mechanized farming is unskillfully applied to light tropical soil, it can disimprove it rapidly. In the accompanying table we see the total area of land in hectares (1 hectare = 2.47 acres) which could be cultivated by tractor in 1953.[1]

Far East	8,500
Near East	1,200
Latin America	470
U.S.S.R.	230
Europe	104
Oceania	100
North America	50

We should also note that in the underdeveloped countries a tractor runs up against innumerable snags. Machinery which is too roughly used wears out quickly, spare parts are difficult to obtain, repair shops are few and far between, and many of the available mechanics are incompetent.

THE ILLUSION OF VAST AVAILABLE AREAS

Another obstacle to agricultural development is that such a low proportion of the total land available is cultivated or cultivable. Anyone who has flown over vast tropical expanses

[1] FAO, *The State of Food and Agriculture, 1955: Review of a Decade and Outlook* (Rome, September, 1955). See Supplement 1, *Recent Developments in the World Food and Agriculture Situation* (Rome, October, 1955).

in an airplane has been amazed to see such huge tracts of desert.

Thus in Black Africa the percentage of cultivated land is low. In Tanganyika, for example, which is representative of much of East Africa, the proportion of cultivated land in 1931 (there has been no noticeable increase since then) was below 1 per cent. Morocco, which was formerly a French protectorate, has 12.5 million acres with a low yield and 17.5 million acres of impoverished in-between land to support its human and animal population. France, whose population is 4 times as large, has 7 times as much land under cultivation and its yield is, in general, 3 or 4 times as high.

The wide open spaces which are the subject of so much speculation are often mythical. What can Egypt do, sandwiched in between two sandy deserts? Or Peru, where crops can be grown only at high altitudes? Chile, whose countryside is marked out like a lunar landscape? Brazil, with the great Amazon basin region where the land is still not settled?

The cost of making these areas productive is often so prohibitive that it is impossible ever to imagine it happening. It is the same where the systematic reforestation of bare slopes is concerned.

Even on level or only slightly hilly ground, extensive cultivation can quickly expose the soil to erosion and salinity. And even in the most favorable circumstances, there is always the problem of the cost of imported mechanical equipment.

Maurice Lengellé has written:

If the underdeveloped countries want eventually to provide for the optimum needs of their populations, they will certainly be forced to follow the example set by Western countries and become the owners of their own agricultural implement factories, sources of fertilizer and fuel oil.[2]

This is relatively easy to say, but in fact how many of the underdeveloped countries, still without the elementary substructures necessary, would be able to accomplish this?

THE IRRATIONAL USE OF LAND

It frequently happens, particularly in Latin America, that huge areas of land are under the control of landowners who are not favorably disposed towards intensive farming or cultivation of any kind. Thousands of acres populated only by wandering herds, or completely gone out of use, are so obvious a scandal that the responsibility for agrarian reform must be placed at the door of these owners.

The I.B.R.D. (International Bank for Reconstruction and Development) experts have given a clear picture of this characteristically Latin American anomaly:

In Latin America, where huge ranches used primarily for grazing predominate, it is impossible to develop food-growing schemes and in this way to satisfy the needs of the urban or even of the rural population. There is a shortage of milk-based products throughout Latin America which could be remedied by concentrating on reproductive animals while paying greater attention to the condition of the soil and by using pasture land in a more rational way. Some Latin American countries, whose population is almost entirely rural and which have a vast acreage of land at their disposal, have to import food for their urban

[2] Maurice Lengellé in *Le Tiers Monde, op. cit.* p. 220.

population, when in fact they could obtain at least part of this on the spot by putting fallow land under the plough. In Venezuela for example, large tracts of fertile land quite near the capital are at the moment extensively used for grazing. If they were worked in a different way however, they could be transformed into truck farms to supply Caracas with vegetables. In other areas food harvested where farming is carried on intensively or on the less fertile slopes in hilly country, has to be brought to the city by porters or pack animals through fertile land where cultivation is less intensively practiced. The land therefore is being used in exactly the opposite way to that which the possibilities of outlet and natural resources would seem to demand.[3]

LOW CAPACITY FOR INVESTMENT

Large investments have to be made to set up agricultural development programs. In developed countries this money comes mainly from the savings of the farmers themselves and in loans from specialized commercial or agricultural banks and from credit organizations which are not reserved to large business undertakings. The substructures have already been established by public enterprise.

The situation in the underdeveloped countries is very different. While Denmark alone, with a population of 4½ million, was able to devote 600 million dollars to agriculture between 1946 and 1954, India, with a population of almost 450 million, was unable to invest more than 200 million dollars in the first three years of her five-year plan (1951–1953), and approximately 1.5 million dollars for irrigation, power, transport and communications, and the social ser-

[3] *The Basis of a Development Program for Colombia* (Washington, D.C., 1950), p. 63.

vices. In Japan the amount of public funds devoted to agriculture, forests and fisheries was increased, during the years between 1948 and 1952, to 392 million dollars. Of this 98 million was invested directly by the State and the remainder was provided in the form of subsidies or loans granted to farmers by the government. In Egypt the amount to be spent on agriculture for the years 1952–1953 to 1955–1956 was increased to 4.4 million dollars.

MONEY-LENDING PRODUCTS

The majority of the farmers in the underdeveloped countries lead miserable lives and can only exist through loans. But the existing credit organizations are not tailored to the needs of the small farmer. The interest rate is so high that in some cases the land given as security for the loan is appropriated, to the benefit of the money-lenders.

The UN report on agricultural reform denounces the callousness and avariciousness of these money-lenders, and analyses the effects of insufficient credit on a short-term basis:

Since these loans have been obtained chiefly to buy food, and since they are given at such a high rate of interest, farmers are generally not in a position to clear their debts and have no alternative but to transfer part or all of their holdings to the person who has lent them the money. In this way, they are reduced to the status of farm workers, or of farmers who do not own land. This growing concentration of property in the hands of the money-lenders is particularly noticeable in southeast Asia, where it was considerably accelerated by the fall in prices during the 1930's. The classic example is to be found in Burma, where money-lenders from the Chettiyar and other communities have financed the expansion of rice-growing in Lower Burma since the end of the 19th century and the beginning of the 20th. During the agricultural crisis the proportion of the total cultivated acreage owned by the Chettiyars in 13 of Lower Burma's principal rice-growing areas rose from 6 per cent in 1930 to 25 per cent in 1937; and the proportion of land which belonged to money-lenders who were not farmers, increased from 19 to 50 per cent in the same period. The same tendency has been evident in India for many years, and also in the countries of the Middle East: a great number of large estates have been built up through the indebtedness of the fellahs.[4]

In India big landowners who want a mortgage can obtain loans at a rate which varies between 9 and 12 per cent in the majority of the provinces. But the small farmers, who form the great bulk of the borrowers, must pay, for guaranteed loans, between 12 and 50 per cent interest. In the case of non-guaranteed loans, they may have to pay as much as 300 per cent. The normal interest rate, in the 16 villages where we carried out a survey in Vietnam, was between 5 and 25 per cent per month.

A cure for usury can, no doubt, be found in credit cooperatives, but in countries where the majority of the people are illiterate and particularly poor, it would be very hard to set up the kind of security which would be necessary.

OTHER DIFFICULTIES

Difficulties that signify even more the insecurity in which farmers live must be commented on as well. Agriculture is exposed to a certain number of natural risks. These assume

[4] UN, *Agricultural Reform* (New York, 1951).

even graver proportions in the underdeveloped countries, owing to natural conditions as much as to the primitive methods used to cope with them.

Aridity is a common complaint in the Middle and Far East, in Africa and in Eastern Europe. Flooding constitutes perhaps an even greater danger to livestock, crops and property in the Far East.

In China the famous Yellow River has overflowed its banks 51 times in 83 years between 1855 and 1938. In India the average acreage of land under flood water has been about 1,500,000 acres and the number of people affected about 900,000. The severe Yangtse floods in 1931 inundated almost 165 million acres and affected 2,527,700 families. The destructive nature of the Ganges, Indus, Mekong, and Menam rivers is equally well known.

Inadequate warehousing and transport frequently mean that harvests rot in one place while famine strikes in another.

The growth of markets on a world-wide scale, while it has done away with some of the inconvenient aspects of localized trade, exposes the farmers and other primary producers of food to the fluctuations of world price levels which, as we know, are much more marked in the case of primary products than in the case of manufactured goods, and more marked than the fluctuations of prices in general.

Such an accumulation of data may seem wearisome and unimpressive to those who have never made a thorough analysis of the needs and the potentialities of the underdeveloped countries. Anyone who loves mankind and has worked in countries where hunger is rife sees it as possessing all the tragedy of a harrowing drama.

7

Obstacles to Industrial Development

*Insufficient transport and power, lack of sufficient
staff and qualified man-power, the absence of a
home market, scarcity of large-scale investment,
these are all obstacles which hinder the industrialization of the underdeveloped countries.*

If the difficulties encountered in agricultural improvement
in underdeveloped countries are considerable, the relative
difficulties in industrialization are even more so. The Department of Economic and Social Affairs in the United Nations
has clearly analyzed these problems.[1]

Here we follow very closely this extremely reliable analysis
which corresponds to our observations. Some remarks on
the sources of power have been added.

SHORTAGES IN THE ECONOMIC FRAMEWORK

In order of importance these are:
1. The inadequacy of the essential economic factors.

[1] UN, *Processes and Problems of Industrialization in Under-Developed Countries* (December, 1954).

2. The imbalance in the development of the different economic sectors.

3. The lack of an adequate home market.

The Inadequacy of Essential Economic Factors

a) The lack of transport facilities hinders the establishment of factories outside the city areas, as they are cut off from easy access to ports of embarkation for their goods to outside markets. The result is a concentration in the urban areas, which is both excessive and overburdening.

b) The shortage or unavailability of power, as well as of means of transport, generally calls for important investment *en bloc*. These essential services cannot be extended progressively as the need for them arises. They have to be created as distinct units of production which are technically complete and often extremely expensive. In such a situation, therefore, the initial amounts of capital invested will anticipate the demand, and when the services created in this way become the center of an economic complex, they will meet the needs of the whole less and less. This transition from the under- to the over-utilization of these services during the course of development constitutes a very delicate problem for the public authorities. Inconsiderate investment of capital in them over and above the probable future demand can waste resources which could have been utilized with greater profit in other sectors of the economy.

c) The lack of industries to use by-products makes the foundation of basic industries a more risky affair.

d) The lack of institutions where skilled labor can be trained and capital mobilized, increases considerably the strain on those undertakings which should in fact benefit from them.

e) The irregular supply of some raw materials and the shortage of spare parts force industrial units to burden themselves with expensive stocks, which would be completely unnecessary in developed countries.

Imbalance between Economic Sectors

Coexistence between a major subsistence economy and a growing economy based on trade, produces a series of deceptive imbalances, social as well as economic. The initial investments in the substructure or in industry modify the very structure of the economic milieu. Industrial enterprises which are called on to play a major role during the first stage of development are those which produce goods for mass consumption. If one or several sectors of the economy do not develop at the same rate as the others, the market remains too limited and this handicaps business which cannot, because of this, develop to the optimum point which would enable it to establish a minimum cost price.

Furthermore, capital can be more easily attracted to the less essential sectors of the economy, such as building luxury apartment houses to meet the needs of a small number of people who command a high income. On the social level many important sectors of the people remain less productive, less adaptable and poorer than the favored sectors.

The Home Market Is Inadequate

On this third point many difficulties arise. There are countries which are often too small to allow secondary industries to reach viable proportions. There are countries where only a tiny fraction of the population has a high enough income, where there is a preference for cheap, mediocre quality products, where many communities are more or less isolated, far away from the commercial centers, and where there is a practical impossibility of finding outlets abroad to make up for the deficiencies of the domestic market.

THE SOCIAL SITUATION

Social obstacles must be added to those of a purely economic nature. The social situation, in its various aspects, does not favor the progress of the underdeveloped countries, which do not benefit in effect from the elements which have made Europe's industrial advance possible.

In societies which have not yet been industrialized, the majority of the population is grouped in rural collective structures whose traditional form (enclosed familial economy and general educational level) does not prepare its individual members for the task of assuming the management of an industrial undertaking. The recruitment of captains of industry therefore tends to be limited to the upper classes, which in any case can provide only a few who are efficient. Even among the upper classes aptitude for becoming a "businessman" is hindered by a scale of values and a way of life which does not encourage individuals to involve themselves in industry.

Insofar as the businessman or industrialist considers his activity not so much as an end in itself, but as a way of improving his social standing, he runs the risk of failing to consider his business as a permanent one, and of hesitating when it comes to involving himself in undertakings whose benefits will only be evident in the long term. These men prefer ordinary commercial transactions or speculative operations.

The low educational level in the majority of underdeveloped countries is without doubt a much more serious obstacle to industrial development than illiteracy was in Europe at the beginning of the industrial era, when techniques were much simpler than they are today.

Health is another factor. Ill-health continues to accentuate the tendency to absenteeism. The intensity of "crowd" diseases does not favor the concentrated, persevering and combined effort on which the productivity of a factory depends.

We also have to take into account the instability prevalent in some new ranks of the working class population, who are not only affected by homesickness, but are continually changing their jobs in the hope of getting a better one.

Finally, it should be noted that the excess revenue of the privileged minority in the underdeveloped countries is frequently dissipated in ostentatious living, in the purchase of land which will not be worked in the best way, in the acquisition of livestock more for prestige than for anything else, in speculation, and in hoarding hard currency, or in investing it safely in the particularly well-developed countries.

To these social factors hampering full productivity must be added the weakness of the public administration. This is evident first of all in the incompetence of generally underpaid officials, and also in the lack of statistical data or the delay in their publication. It is further evident in the arbitrary nature of government decisions, and in the existence of a right of expropriation which the state occasionally reserves.

RESTRICTIONS ON THE INTERNATIONAL LEVEL

In *Limitations Imposed by the International Situation*,[2] the UN has pointed out three kinds of obstacles to development.

1. The underdeveloped countries are dependent on the developed countries for the supply of equipment. In addition, they are unable to obtain these at all if the developed countries are in the process of reconstruction following a war, or if they do not possess the necessary currency.

It is also apposite to point out that, owing to the progress made in the provision of plant and apparatus in the developed countries, the materials they are able to supply do not meet the requirements of the underdeveloped countries, which are in a different phase of development.

2. The developed countries impose various restrictions on the modernization of industry in the less developed countries.

This is also evident in the restriction of patents where pressure is brought to bear on commercial, financial or transportation undertakings to impede the development of local industries in order to reduce the amount of competition or to encourage "dumping."

3. The developed countries frequently place an embargo

[2] *Ibid.*

on the export of the capital sums necessary to help the industrialization of the underdeveloped countries.

AVAILABLE SOURCES OF POWER

Without going into a detailed analysis of the various kind of obstacles, it will be sufficient if we examine in this section a few statistics relating to the sources of power available in the underdeveloped countries.

If we take 1 kilowatt as equalling 750 grams of coal, 2,250 grams of lignite, 400 grams of petroleum-based products, or half a cubic meter of natural gas, *Le Tiers Monde* suggests that figures for available energy in 1950 were, per year and per inhabitant, less than 100 kilowatts in India and Indonesia, approximately 150 in China and Africa, and 240 in Latin America. The figures for the United States, Great Britain and Germany were 5,000 kilowatts or over.

In 1952 the United States consumed 35.9 per cent of all the power used in the world, Western Europe consumed 19 per cent, Eastern Europe and the U.S.S.R., 17.2 per cent. The total for the underdeveloped countries reached only 18.9 per cent; 13.4 per cent of this in Asia, 3 per cent in Latin America and 1.4 per cent in Africa (excepting the South African Republic).

These few figures, together with the information already given, will be sufficient to show the magnitude of the obstacles facing industrialization in the majority of the semi-developed countries and in every single one of the underdeveloped countries.

8

Obstacles to Technical Progress

There is no technical progress without cultural progress.

Technical development cannot take place unless it is accompanied by corresponding progress in the field of education. Technical progress presupposes a certain fairly high standard of literacy, post-primary education for a large proportion of the adolescent population, the availability of competent teachers in the specialized higher institutes of learning, and finally a certain concentration of industry.

These conditions are not found—or exist to too slight a degree—in the underdeveloped countries which suffer in effect from a three-fold handicap:

1) An educational handicap;
2) Inadequate supply of men to fill higher posts in industry;
3) Inadequate cultural and economic integration.

THE EDUCATIONAL HANDICAP

Some figures—which should not be taken as absolute—will nevertheless define the outlines of this question. They demonstrate that there are whole groups of people who have never attended school and do not know how to read (see Table 5).[1]

While the number of children attending school is rising as a whole, the number of illiterates—more than 500 million in 1962—is also growing.

TABLE 5

Proportion of Illiterates over Ten Years of Age
(*per cent*)

1. *Near East and Far East*

Iran	40	Malaya	62
Philippines	40	Korea	69
Ceylon	42	Turkey	70
Hong Kong	49	Pakistan	86
China	55	British Borneo	90
Thailand	60	India	92
Burma	60	Indonesia	92

2. *Africa*

Uganda	70	Egypt	85
Sierra Leone	71	Nyasaland	93
Ghana	80	Mozambique	99

3. *Latin America*

Chile	28	Brazil	57
Puerto Rico	30	El Salvador	60
Panama	35	Nicaragua	63
Colombia	44	Guatemala	65
Mexico	52	Honduras	66
Ecuador	55	Bolivia	80
Peru	57		

[1] L.–J. Lebret, A. Piettre, A. Sauvy, and R. Delprat, *Niveaux de vie, besoins et civilisation* (Paris: Editions Ouvrières, 1956). See Appendix I, Statistical Tables, pp. 169–178.

Literacy does not mean simply education. When you examine the educational statistics for the underdeveloped countries, you can see that a high percentage of children are not "enrolled," but that many who are enrolled never attend school. You can also see that there is considerable absenteeism among those who do attend, that the duration of the primary school cycle is very short, and that very few children complete it.

An analysis of the teaching staffs also shows that they are often under strength both numerically and intellectually. There are too few teacher training colleges for men and women, and therefore "occasional" teachers, usually unqualified, have to be enlisted. These are then put in charge of overcrowded classes, one half of which may come to school in the morning and the other half in the afternoon.

Educational programs furthermore lean far too heavily on those of the developed countries for their inspiration. Teaching is not geared to everyday reality, and does not help to prepare students to deal with the actual tasks peculiar to their own countries.

The result of this is that a large proportion of the labor force, even if it is manually and mentally alert, cannot rise above the level of the unskilled worker. Specialization and higher qualifications become more difficult or even impossible to achieve. Where it is a question of leaders of industry, some idea of the caliber of the people who can be called upon to take part in development work in their native countries, can be obtained by examining the figures for attendance at institutes of higher education given in a UN report.[2]

2 UN, *Preliminary Report on the World Social Situation* (September, 1952).

In North America (the United States and Canada) about one person in 75 followed a course of higher education in 1949–1950.

In Europe, the proportion was 1 in 350.

In Latin America, 1 in 725.

In the Middle East, 1 in 1,250.

In Asia, it appears to be approximately 1 in 1,100 or 1 in 1,200; but the variations between different countries are too wide for us to assume that this average has any validity.

The proportion of students from the autonomous countries of Africa (Egypt and South Africa excluded), including those who attend institutes of higher education abroad, probably does not exceed 1 out of every 20,000 inhabitants. The inter-African conference on Higher Education, in its concluding report, aims at an increase from 31,000 to 274,000 by 1980.

THE SHORTAGE OF EXECUTIVES

Many technicians who have attended institutes of higher education will, in spite of this, lack the qualities necessary in an executive.

In the underdeveloped countries the small proportion of men who are capable of establishing and directing enterprises leads the government to take the place of private initiative.

It can of course happen in the underdeveloped countries that some men who display initiative and enterprise rise to the top. But at the same time, anyone who is attempting to move from the working class into the managerial class runs the risk of being swamped by details at the moment of transition. He will want to keep everything under his control at all times, direct and guide events, including the most insignificant details, while at the same time he forgets the need to create the proper executive staff to allow himself to dominate the technical and commercial evolution of his business.

Furthermore, the underdeveloped countries, if they want to dominate the integrated evolution of their economies, find themselves forced to establish nationalized industries to make up for the deficiencies in private initiative, and establish planning organizations for which they cannot call on a sufficient number of experts. They are therefore forced to call in experts from abroad whose tour of duty is often too short to be of any real value. Research or planning organizations, furthermore, lack the authority necessary to ensure that their recommendations are put into practice. Sometimes too people in charge of these establishments are too often changed with change of government; and occasionally they have not received a technical training or have not been sufficiently briefed. Every innovation attracts their enthusiasm; one project follows another; grandiose schemes grind to a halt for lack of funds, and appeals for foreign aid do not meet with the desired response.

THE DIFFICULTIES OF CULTURAL AND ECONOMIC INTEGRATION

The third point to which we must draw attention is that concerning the difficulties of cultural and economic integration in the underdeveloped countries.

Forced technical development may seem desirable to

some; in fact, it multiplies human degradation and social contradictions.

In the light of what has been said, one can understand the difficulties facing the underdeveloped countries and *a fortiori* the non-developed countries, when it comes to creating the "technical atmosphere" necessary for rapid industrialization—even at an elementary level in the case of the underdeveloped countries—or to establishing precision industries in the already more developed countries. The number of people who can manage a modern, or, to an even greater extent, a precision industry, is very low. The success that has attended some projects can be ascribed to the exceptional quality of a few executives, often from abroad, who themselves have been able to train personnel both for management and for labor.

This explains why industrialization in the underdeveloped countries tends to be concentrated in the large cities which are already industrialized to a considerable extent. Sao Paulo, in Brazil, is the most typical example of this.

Only in those cities where the technical atmosphere has already been created, can one find a labor force that has evolved to the point where it can assume responsibility for operations that demand additional professional qualities. Apprenticeship schools are more numerous, and technicians are encouraged to keep abreast of current developments in their fields rather than allowed to become "rusty."

But the great industrial cities, developing at such a very rapid rate, attract a considerable number of unqualified workers whose professional education would take at least a generation and who form a kind of sub-proletariat, sometimes passive and sometimes unruly.

9

The Financial and Economic Obstacles

The economy of the underdeveloped countries is always vulnerable, and always depends upon that of the advanced countries.

ECONOMIC OBSTACLES

An underdeveloped economy is vulnerable. When it is subjected to the give–and–take of international trade, it suffers violent setbacks. Any imbalance in world trade makes itself felt throughout the country, where it combines with the already existing domestic imbalance to produce a fatal inflationary tendency.

International Economy and the Underdeveloped Countries

The underdeveloped countries are at a disadvantage in their dealings with the more developed countries. They have to import a wide variety of goods, while their range of exports is very limited (usually agricultural produce and raw materials). Therefore, if the price of any one of these commodities fluctuates, it has considerable repercussions on

74

the entire economy. These fluctuations nullify all attempts at long-term forecastings and consequently all long-term economic planning. About 63 per cent of Ghana's economy, for example, is based on the price of cacao. Some 99 per cent of Gambia's exports consist of ground-nuts, and 95 per cent of Northern Rhodesia's exports are of metal and minerals. Finally, 78 per cent of Nyasaland's exports are tobacco and tea.

As an underdeveloped country has to import all its technical equipment and industrial goods, it depends principally on its exports for revenue. One can see how difficult a situation an underdeveloped country would be in if the price of its principal export suddenly falls, as has happened in Ghana, for example. It can also be appreciated how an underdeveloped country can, because of this, be at the mercy of the dominant economy of its largest customer.

This sort of situation exemplifies the vulnerability and insecurity of the underdeveloped countries. In fact, their position becomes even worse as the rate of exchange deteriorates. The "rate of exchange" is a term used to describe the relationship between the price index of exports and the similar index for imports at any given moment. An economic analysis of the situation, therefore, shows that over and above the annual fluctuations which may be to either the advantage or disadvantage of the underdeveloped countries, there is a distinct tendency for the rate of exchange to deteriorate in the long run, to the detriment of the underdeveloped countries. In other words, the grip of poverty is tightened; the resources of the underdeveloped countries are continually diminishing even though their rate of production may remain constant or even increase. Now, even if the trend were in the other direction (and therefore favorable), the yield from their exports would still be insufficient to ensure their economic growth.

The Internal Economy of the Underdeveloped Countries: Fatality of Inflation

Analysis of the internal economy of the underdeveloped countries once more shows us clearly the nature of the vicious circle of poverty which hems them in. The fluctuations of exchange and deterioration of the rate of exchange aggravate the internal imbalance and provoke a fatal inflationary crisis.

During boom periods when demand increases, the re-entry of money can increase at such a rate that even control measures become incapable of halting inflation. The improvement in trade tends to provoke an increase in the volume of consumer goods—and very often of luxury goods—and encourages investment trends which never, or very rarely, contribute to economic progress. In many cases, because of the precarious nature of the increase in the price paid for exports, it proves difficult to allot these receipts so that they will be utilized in the best interests of the country. A major part of this revenue, too, may be sent out of the country. Even when certain investment projects are given top priority, they are sometimes launched on so large a scale that they cannot possibly last when prosperity on the export market is replaced by depression.

During a recession the reduction in the value of exports and the deficit in the balance of payments lead to the devaluation of money or the limitation of imports. State revenue depends to a great extent on indirect taxation, including taxes on exports. When revenue is sharply reduced, it is difficult to reduce expenditure by the same amount. New methods of payment are therefore created.

This difficulty presents the same problem when, because of high estimates or altered trading methods, an underdeveloped country whose public revenue is largely based on customs taxes on incoming goods, finds itself forced to reduce imports significantly or considerably without being able to avoid the necessity for issuing bank notes to ensure the continued functioning of the administration and the execution, however impeded, of its land development program.

It is clear from this analysis that the development of backward countries meets multiple obstacles whose dangers are not always recognized by their rulers. The difficulties of planned development are considerable even for those countries which have consistently strong exports.

FINANCIAL PROBLEMS

Underdeveloped countries lack the capital funds necessary to ensure their industrial and agricultural development. This is one of the basic obstacles to progress. To ensure decisive economic advance in Asia, accompanied by a significant increase in the standard of living, really enormous investments—amounting to about twice the national revenue of the U.S.A.—would be needed!

In reality, then, investment is ridiculously insufficient. In effect:

1) Savings account for only a very small proportion of the national revenue (5 per cent in countries which are

beginning to be developed, as against 15 per cent in the more developed countries). And the national revenue itself is extremely low when it is compared with that in developed countries. For example, 5 per cent savings on an income of between 50 and 100 dollars per person is equivalent to between $2.50 and $5, while 15 per cent savings on an income of between 500 and 1,500 dollars is equivalent to between $75 and $225. The investment capacity of an underdeveloped country, therefore, is 10 times or 100 times less, per inhabitant, than in a developed country.

2) These savings are concentrated in the hands of a limited number of people.

3) Much of the funds are sent out of the country or hoarded.

4) A great deal is tied up in speculative dealings.

5) Investments made with a view to profit only have no effect on the most important activities being carried on in both the public and private sectors of the economy.

6) A reasoned choice of investments is impossible without the help of research groups or planning organizations, which at the moment either do not exist or, if they do, can call on the services of too few competent specialists. The result of this is that investment in basic industries or in industries which process raw material is slowed down by the absence of substructures. Or else the effort expended in providing the substructure is so considerable that there is no financial margin left over to provide directly productive equipment.

As a result of this, the balance of development cannot be achieved. And poverty, far from decreasing, spreads its wings even wider.

10

Sociological Obstacles

The best equipment will remain unproductive if it is not under the control of competent men who work in an atmosphere which is both receptive to innovation and conducive to progress.

The social conditions required for cultural and economic development are rarely present in backward countries. This is the case, for example, in an undeveloped area where there is familial and tribal resistance to new ways of life, where the influences of witch-doctors or traditional religious practices have to be countered, and where a proliferation of sects which oppose each other or the dominant religion all give rise to difficulties which militate against a rational and coordinated development program. The advantages of development clearly seem to outweigh other considerations, but personal beliefs are normally of long duration and are not easily put aside or forgotten.

The same difficulties are frequently encountered in the still tribal marginal areas of underdeveloped countries. In such countries the obstacles to rapid and balanced development are: widespread illiteracy; a disinclination for progress and the poor quality of leadership; the existence of tyranny

79

or of a democracy which is democratic only in name, the control being exercised by powerful families who exploit the rest of the people; strife between parties which have, in some cases, been at loggerheads for centuries; the proliferation of parties which lack any ideology (frequently composed of the numerous hangers-on of an adventurer or of someone who is merely ambitious); and a concept of society in which a self-styled aristocratic class believes that it alone matters in public affairs.

The difficulties caused by the transition from rural to urban life, by concealed unemployment, by a way of life which favors fantasy rather than the rigid discipline of industrial work, are encountered throughout the whole economy.

Then in both the country and the towns there are the marginal "sub-populations" who are always backward. Frequently too, social programs are too ambitious, too difficult, ill-conceived, or badly carried out.

When the middle classes begin to emerge, they are seized by a desire to live ostentatiously; and this encourages them to enrich themselves by any means so that the life they lead will approximate that led by the original ruling classes, and which will divide them from the still backward millions. The selfishness of these new population groups is no less than the selfishness of the long-established ruling classes. The study of the distribution of the national income, whenever it is statistically possible, demonstrates that between 60 and 80 per cent of the national wealth is owned and spent by between 5 and 20 per cent of the people.

In this chapter we will consider only some of the social aspects of the most significant difficulties to be encountered.

JUXTAPOSED BUT UNCOORDINATED STRUCTURES

As Raymond Barre emphasizes, Nurske had good reason for saying that "the progress of the underdeveloped countries is much more than just an economic problem."[1]

It is because they have ignored or neglected this fact that ambitious economic development programs have only had misleading results. The most perfect equipment will be useless if it is not handled by competent men in an atmosphere which encourages innovation and breathes optimism.

Certain ideologies have to be searchingly examined and some illusions have to be abandoned. The growth of the underdeveloped countries is considerably impeded by certain flaws inherent in their social structure. All groups in the society are unbalanced and disjointed. For the most part, between an administrative or landed aristocracy and the wretched masses there are few intermediary social groups capable of providing dynamic political and economic leadership. Political institutions are unstable and ill-adapted. When one thinks of the degree of planning which these countries need, the introduction of normal parliamentary democracy in an unqualified and unsuitable form would seem to be fatal.

All economic development must find a place within the social organism. Two different attitudes are, in effect, tenable with regard to the development of the backward countries. The first would be that of the engineer who attends to the mechanical and technological aspect of things and ignores the rest. The second is that of the biologist who knows that the plant develops cell by cell in accordance with the laws of its own nature, and

[1] Regnar Nurske, *Problems of Capital Formation in Under-Developed Countries* (Oxford: Blackwell, 1953), p. 157.

within the limits laid down by its origins and environment. Only the latter attitude is realistic.[2]

ALARMING ASPECTS OF URBAN CONCENTRATION

One of the most alarming aspects of this evolution, as we see it taking place rapidly before our very eyes, is the disorganized concentration of people in urban areas. This has serious implications for mankind.

Singapore, for instance, suffers from its enormous size. As in other countries, there is a chaotic and unbalanced metropolis which has developed in an irregular and improvised way. The population has nearly doubled in 20 years. Hong Kong's population, 800,000 strong in 1931, is now estimated at more than 3 million. In these circumstances, it is obvious that both cities suffer from a considerable degree of over-population, and that part of the population lives in hovels. This poses serious problems of hygiene, notably those concerned with the campaign against tuberculosis.

Anyone who has travelled through the underdeveloped parts of the world has seen any number of similar cases, even in the still relatively unimportant towns where a more or less modern central quarter is surrounded by a belt of primitive or improvised dwellings.

We cannot, however, avoid urbanization; but because of shortsighted politicians and technicians who are unable to appreciate the human factor responsible for it, we are well on the way to creating a decisive social backwardness in these communities.

[2] Raymond Barre in *Critique* (December, 1954).

International experts are not always sufficiently aware of this. They approach this delicate problem in the light of their own ideas of what will produce the best of all possible worlds; and when they are faced with the essential question they are content to answer it with evasions, inadequately worked out solutions, or hypothetical remedies.

It is clear that the beginnings of industrialization and entry into the field of international trade signify the creation of material values, some of which are genuinely valuable, and others of which destroy certain traditional cultural values. It must be acknowledged that until now neither the West, dominated by the need to satisfy its growing demands, nor the underdeveloped countries, forced to try to achieve in a few years the same results as the West has achieved after several centuries, have been able to find the formulae for harmonious evolution.

THE LIMITS OF SOCIAL EFFORT

The developed countries, faced with the social evils created by their industrialization, have reacted progressively by increasing the numbers of social institutions and by increasing public expenditure in the social sector of the economy. Their capacity for production enables them to do this. But this is not the case in the insufficiently developed countries. In a country where the national income is $500 per inhabitant, expenditure on social services does not exceed $50 per person; in a country where the national income is $100 per person, the amount spent on social services is on the level of $4 or $5 per person.

If one were to break down the expenditure needed in the

educational sector of the economy, for example, and ascertain the extent of the urgent need for school equipment, buildings, and teachers, one would be astonished by the amount of money which would have to be set aside to meet this single need.

Let us assume first of all that in the advanced countries the percentage of the total population between 5 and 14 years old is appreciably lower than in the underdeveloped countries. The difference is sometimes in the ratio 1 to 2. This phenomenon is essentially due to the recent decrease in the infant mortality rate of the underdeveloped countries.

The only way in which the underdeveloped countries can meet their commitments is by supplying rudimentary installations and half-trained educational personnel. It is the same where hospital equipment is concerned.

Alfred Sauvy has given us a very clear impression of the impasse in which the developed countries—which will still have to support the rapidly increasing underdeveloped populations—will find themselves from now on.

Let us suppose that President Bourguiba has to build schools and finds himself gravely embarrassed financially. He will install makeshift classes in an old building, possibly even in an Arab hut. The teacher's intelligence will doubtless leave something to be desired; but eventually he will manage to teach the alphabet and elementary mathematics to children who will be seated on stones or tree trunks. If we are to build schools, we cannot provide modern classrooms for the French, at a cost of some 6 or 8 million Old Francs each, and rudimentary classrooms for the Moslems, still less two different salary scales for the teachers.[3]

[3] Alfred Sauvy, "Quelques données réalistes du probléme algérien," *Le Monde* (May 11, 1957).

Now we touch on the principal problem of homogeneous development in the underdeveloped countries. Since their ambitions approximate those of the developed countries, the effort they expend on one enterprise prevents them from making progress on all fronts.

We can imagine the difficulties—not only technological and social, but psychological as well—that have to be overcome in order to effect a reasonably coordinated development program in the underdeveloped countries. This is because it frequently happens that men who suddenly climb to positions of power have no inherent superiority other than that embodied in their desire to dominate. Lacking social and economic culture, lacking study centers capable of analyzing situations, resources and needs, and occasionally motivated by the desire to enlarge their own assets considerably, these men yield more to impulse than to reason, and to the temptation of doing things for effect rather than for the sake of progressive, balanced development.

What is big attracts them more than what is necessary; and the assertion of a central authority seems more attractive to them than spontaneous and lasting cooperation between population groups. They certainly try to create enthusiasm, but enthusiasm for themselves personally rather than the sort of enthusiasm that will ensure that the overall design is successfully accomplished. Large, expensive projects remain unfinished; and one can see that the programs which have been completed are neither adapted to the urgent needs of the country nor proportionate to the resources available. The electricity from a huge hydroelectric project will not be used; a network of roads will be neglected; a railway may run uselessly beside a canal or a river; ports may be created where there is no productive hinterland or where they are unusable because of uncontrollable silting; or, further still, huge tracts of forest are marked down for lumbering before anyone has reckoned the cost of the communications system needed to serve them.

Part Three

The Situation in the World Today:
CONCLUSION

We have analyzed here the basic premises of the under-developed countries' position. Their tragic plight has been made clear. Multiple difficulties prevent them from achieving economic growth on their own. Humanity has never before been faced with a series of problems as difficult to solve as those which are created by the success of the campaign to reduce infant mortality and extend life expectancy. Most moderate estimates allow for a population of at least 5 billion human beings by the end of the century. It is possible that the figure will even be as high as 6 billion. It is not merely the problem of clothing and feeding people—they have to be housed and taught as well.

This problem becomes even more serious in the light of the discovery that about three-quarters of the human race are either strictly speaking undernourished or deprived of the essential protective foods.

World agricultural production will have to be almost tripled at least by the end of the century in order to ensure adequate supplies for the minimum population forecasted. Moreover, this production will have to be distributed in such a way that everyone has a sufficient share of it.

The situation is such, in effect, that the tripling of the world's agricultural production, which would be possible if a great coordinated effort were made, cannot be achieved simply by an increase in the cultivated acreage or in the average yield. Many areas are already extremely over-populated, and the soil in other areas is rapidly deteriorating. Cultivable areas are used widely for grazing; other areas which could provide all the food needed to support their own population, are devoted instead to industrial or agricultural production for export. Settlers open up new lands, but pay no attention to the need to preserve them. Capital funds needed to ensure effective agricultural development are devoted to speculation. If the present tendencies are maintained, mankind will scarcely dent the impact of hunger. Supposing that, thanks to large-scale transportation of food and other commodities, they reach the required calorific level, the situation will nevertheless still exist in which the majority of the world's population will have less than the normal minimum amount of proteins of animal origin, vitamins and mineral salts.

Apart from small groups of the highly privileged, the majority of people will remain below what is strictly speaking the necessary minimum. The gap between the different social strata will be further accentuated in a great number of underdeveloped countries. But increasing literacy will make the non-privileged peoples become more aggressive towards the privileged members of their own race and also towards those other countries which are better off.

Agricultural and industrial development will only proceed slowly, in absolute terms, in the majority of the underdeveloped countries, as their capacity for saving will continue to be weak; and the appropriations for investment will barely affect the average income per head, which will have been very slightly increased. In contrast, the underdeveloped peoples will lack groups of men capable of directing development on a national, regional or even local scale, and will lack even agricultural workers and properly qualified administrators.

Governments in the underdeveloped countries will yield easily to the temptation of idle show, and will waste a large part of their nations' resources in projects whose value is mainly for prestige, thus making harmonious development impossible.

The difference between the spending power of the least developed peoples and that of the most advanced peoples, as far as it has been possible to estimate it at present, will vary from 1 to 40 to 1 to 100, thus increasing the animosity felt by the under-privileged countries.

The world will therefore be involved in a situation from which it will find it impossible to extricate itself, and one in which the great powers and international organizations will be helpless. The nominal democracies in the underdeveloped countries will conceal successive dictatorships, ill-equipped to resolve internal tensions. There will also be some relatively more powerful nations whose neighbors will influence them towards an imperialist policy of domination.

When the hopes of the masses have been disappointed to such a great extent, the mirage of Communism will exercise an even greater fascination; but Russia will be incapable of undertaking the task of restoring order among a disunited people. The most probable outcome will be anarchical conflict.

These forecasts, which are based strictly on the premises given, are valid, of course, only if present erroneous methods are persisted in, and if the major powers fail to abandon their traditional attitudes. At the same time, even supposing that the leading nations are "converted" to the objective consideration of the world's major problems, there will still be immense difficulties, and they will be only partly overcome.

People are slow to apply psychological know-how and scientific research to these fundamental and urgent questions; and their intellectual commitment to the present-day position of mankind and its contradictions remains (with some rare exceptions) completely rudimentary, if not absolutely childish. We must therefore examine with great care the roles played up to now by different countries in the campaign to develop the world in a more balanced way. We shall be able, after analyzing their mistakes, to formulate the basic factors for what François Perroux has called "a new civilization."

The Demands
Made by a New Civilization

*The tragedy is that the West has, in its
actions, gone back on the scale of values
bequeathed to it by Christianity and
which is today the scale of values that
could inspire a new civilization.*

Part Four

Demands Made by a New Civilization:
THE ATTITUDES OF THE PAST

*The greatest evil in the world is not the
poverty of those who are deprived, but
the unconcern of those who are well off.*

After having exposed with the maximum possible objectivity
(taking the present state of our statistical knowledge into
account) the paradoxical state of humanity when it seeks to
satisfy its needs, we must now show the responsibility of the
privileged Western world in the light of this situation.

I would like to show, first of all, how the downfall of the
colonial empires did not materially modify the seriousness
of the question, because a new form of imperialism is attempting to take the place of its predecessor. However, this
statement is not to be taken as an attack on the major
powers. My intention is solely to examine certain aspects of
humanity's recent history and certain aspects of the evolution which is taking place before our eyes.

In this way we can better discover the errors perpetrated
by capitalism. This economic system, in effect, can exist only
by continually modifying itself to the point where it but
very slightly resembles the original version. By following its

present trend it would be incapable of effecting adequate development all over the world, which would be the only correct response to mankind's unsatisfied hunger.

We can also see how—through unconcern, perhaps more than through selfishness—the West has contributed to the fragmentation of civilizations other than its own and provoked anti-Western revolutions.

However painful this examination happens to be, it is none the less necessary. The West continues to enshrine civilization's greatest values. Our duty is to help the West to recognize them and to disseminate them on the present scale of its sphere of influence which, though it may appear narrow, is in fact wider than it has been up to now.

11

Economic Imperialism

*In the United States 6 per cent of the world's
population consumes 40 per cent of the world's
produce.*

AMERICAN DOMINATION

Since the end of the First, and even more since the end of
the Second World War, British domination over the rest of
the world, which had existed until the end of the nineteenth
and the beginning of the twentieth century, has given place
to domination by America. This has been clearly illustrated
as much by UN documents as by the studies of economists
of the stature of François Perroux in his books *L'Europe
sans rivages* and *La coexistence pacifique*.

Consider the statistics in Table 6 which show to what
extent the United States relies upon exports from other
countries.[1]

It is not difficult to see that this world-wide dependence
on the United States corresponds to the almost exclusive
dependence of the United States on a number of exporting
countries.

[1] *Etudes et Conjoncture* (Paris, Presses Universitaires de France,
December, 1956), pp. 1.172, 1.173.

TABLE 6

Percentage of World Exports Absorbed by the United States

Cane sugar	40	Nickel	70
Coffee	60	Tin	40
Cocoa	40	Zinc	30
Wool	25	Crude oil	20
Silk	30	Iron ore	20
Rubber	40	Newsprint	40
Copper	45	Watches and clocks	50
Lead	60	Glassware	20
Aluminum	20	Ceramics	40

In terms of value the United States attracts one-eighth of the world trade. Its exports represent one-fifth of the world's exports. Reflection on these two figures alone will demonstrate the extent of U.S. domination in the sphere of world trade.

In the course of our analysis of obstacles to development in the backward countries, we noted the complete upheavals that these countries experience owing to the fluctuations of foreign trade. The underdeveloped countries, which export principally raw material and unprocessed foodstuffs, often find that they are very severely affected by even minor disturbances in the American economy. In this way the forces at work in an uncoordinated world lead to economic direction and, eventually, to American domination. This situation is aggravated by the fact that American exports have to be paid for in American dollars.

The expression "free world" disguises a reality in which the world is subservient to American economic power.

No matter how much one admires American prosperity, productivity, and the American virtues, it still induces a kind of vertigo when one considers that the United States, with 6 per cent of the world's population, produces and consumes 40 per cent of the fruits of the earth. The accompanying table, showing the relationship between the consumption of electricity and national income, is significant.

	*Consumption of electricity in 1955 in kilowatt hours per person per year**	*National Income 1952–54 in U.S. dollars*
U.S.A.	2,900	1,870
France	900	740
Japan	500	190
Philippines	40	150
Pakistan	6	65

* The statistics for the highly industrialized countries have greatly increased since this date. The comparative differences between nations, however, still remain largely the same.

THE CRY OF ALARM

A country which dominates the world's economy has grave responsibilities. The United States is not yet fully aware of this. For this reason we should pay attention to Alfred Sauvy's warning, issued more than a decade ago.

The United States can boast of a high national revenue, of record productivity, and even of enviable wage scales for the majority of its people. Nevertheless, in the light of world trends such a policy could easily lose sight of what is happening to the rest of the world, that is, some 94 per cent. Let us leave the

Soviet world out of this in order to emphasize that what we are dealing with is not the antagonism of two rival systems, but a terrible development threatening the heart of a world which yearns to be free.

The most serious reproach levelled at the United States concerns its attitude to the underdeveloped countries. The virtues of "Point IV" are known, but, in the United States, there is an even more pronounced desire, namely, to introduce birth control in the slums of Calcutta or among the huts of the Egyptian *fellaya*. This is to allow the end to justify the means. Because, apart from a few measures, all American policy ultimately aims at preventing these countries from developing. The eminent demographer Notestein said courageously: "In launching a modernization programme, the major powers in the world today would in fact be creating a world in which their own countries would be part of an ever-dwindling minority whose people would control an ever-decreasing proportion of the world's wealth and power."

The United States, which was an exporter of raw material for years, has begun to import it. Its high productivity level is based on economy of man-power, but it involves an incredible waste of materials. Part of its soil has been destroyed; more is being steadily exhausted or eroded. Roosevelt said in 1943: "If there were to be a third world war, we would have to get our fuel from somewhere else." Today huge companies control 75 per cent of the world's petroleum. The Middle East alone has absorbed 25 per cent of all foreign investment since 1945. It is not a question of developing the Middle East, but of getting its petroleum. In the same way the U.S. looks for iron ore from Canada, uranium from the Congo, cobalt from Morocco and so on. The construction of blast furnaces in some parts of South America is impeded if not even prevented.

The annual consumption of steel per inhabitant amounts to more than 1,000 pounds in the U.S., as against 10 pounds in the

Far East. How could the underdeveloped countries manage to consume appreciable quantities of steel which has been smelted in the United States and resold, after machining, at 10 times its original value?

Eisenhower in his election-victory speech set forth unequivocally an American objective: "the provision by the rest of the world, as compensation for the goods with which we supply them, of larger amounts of the raw materials which are not available in sufficient quantity in this country."

This much is quite clear. Internal American waste, and the need to import from abroad, prevent the natural owners of the raw material from using it in the way which would be most beneficial to them.

The consumption of raw material is the same thing as the consumption of the soil. If one-sixteenth of the world's inhabitants, who are already in control of extensive land, consume 60 per cent of the world's raw material, the remaining fifteen-sixteenths must realize that their livelihood is gravely threatened.

And on occasion the waste is enormous. In America 5 million tons of newsprint are used every year, and most of this is devoted to commercial publicity, that is, an attempt to sell other products. Every time the consumption of newsprint rises by 10 per cent in the United States, what is consumed is the raw material that could assist in the instruction of 100 million illiterates elsewhere.

Enterprise is free, but conscience is not.

The cry of warning needed to halt the march of this implacable machine, whose interior productivity is the cause of more and more destruction abroad, can come only from an outsider.[2]

This conclusion, though argued in strong terms, must not be understood as being prompted by any feeling of ill-will towards the United States. Rather do we wish, because of our

[2] Alfred Sauvy in *L'Observateur* (March 26, 1953).

affection for Americans and without minimizing their faults, to offer them this warning. Their universal potential for doing good, if it were objectively applied, would earn them the moral prestige and affectionate recognition that they have not been able to obtain up to now.

12

The Fatal Errors of Capitalism

By virtue of its internal logic capitalism tends towards the profitable rather than to the necessary.

The mistakes made by the original colonialism and the oversights of the new are not so much the mistakes and oversights of individual men as the faults inherent in the system itself. England, France, Portugal, the Netherlands, and Belgium could all prepare copious biographical dictionaries of great Europeans who in the colonies have been loyal soldiers, heroic pioneers, benevolent developers, and honest, able administrators. They have sometimes been men of genius, and have possessed a genuine affection for the people who were at first their subjects but later their allies.

It would be completely unjust to confine oneself to abuse and to refuse to consider all the positive help that the mother countries have accorded their overseas possessions. Anti-colonialist over-simplification is as wide of the mark as any other form of exaggeration. The injustices perpetrated by the recently liberated countries, or by those in revolt against the countries which have allowed them to exist, to grow, and to commence their development, are no less shocking than those of the colonialists who first exploited them. The accession of these re-invigorated nations to a new phase of liberty and progress has been possible only through the assistance that has been forthcoming from the West in the form of measures of hygiene and sanitation, of peace-keeping military forces and engineers, of funds voluntarily raised or otherwise, and, often, of sincere friendship.

The major fault of colonialism has been (as in the European mother countries themselves) the establishment of the proletariat, the inevitable product of the capitalist system, whose increasingly powerful operations tend to dominate the entire framework of trade.

THE INTERNAL LOGIC OF CAPITALISM

It is easy to justify capitalism as a system through which enterprise can be promoted. In a group of people a man emerges who considers that he is capable of organizing the production of a "saleable" (and therefore "useful") article from a labor force which, if it had not been for his intervention, would have remained unemployed or under-employed, and which, even if it were put to work, would not be very productive. This entrepreneur, therefore, as a man who provides work, and produces goods that are "useful," is a benefactor of humanity.

His enterprise, however, has its risks. If the entrepreneur has estimated his needs incorrectly, if he has tried to put too much capital to work, if he has failed to estimate correctly the available market, or if he turns out to be less efficient than his competitors, he finds himself more or less rapidly heading for a fall.

The captains of industry who survive are the better ones, that is to say, those who are most productive and who are most successful in adapting production to need. Their success is legitimate and beneficial.

The argument in defense of capitalism, reduced to its essentials in this way, and without considering the insecurity of the workers and the low standard of living to which they are condemned, has held good throughout the historical period which has seen liberty become reality, and which has witnessed the beginnings of technological progress.

It is still valid in countries where development is in its infancy. The entrepreneurs of Sao Paulo or Porto Alegre in Brazil, those of Medellin or Cali in Colombia, to take only two countries, have set these nations on the road to industrialization. The phase of private enterprise was, as Marx clearly affirmed, a necessary phase, and there is nothing to prove that it will not continue to be so for the supply of certain goods and services. If it is made more humane by certain legal restrictions, it can contribute to a better division of labor, a reduction in waste, an advance in technology, and fuller utilization of resources.

But when a capitalist system develops, many difficulties arise. The organized laboring classes begin to demand social improvements. These demands have to be progressively met by legislation.

Productive countries where wages are high or where social legislation is forward-looking, have more or less escaped the influence of a revolutionary majority which can be fatal to the general utilization of the means of production.

Nevertheless the capitalist system, even within these countries, has undergone far-reaching changes. These may have been made to guarantee certain rights for the workers, or to make up for the deficiencies of free enterprise, or to lessen the disastrous effects of an anarchical rivalry, or perhaps to ensure an overall coordination which has become necessary on a national scale.

The techniques of state intervention in such cases, after earlier ill-adjusted attempts at self-orientation, have been improved and perfected to the point where the entire economy is subjected to a system of planning which is more or less a guided one.

But when the problem no longer concerns merely the effective exploitation of a country where large resources and a technically competent personnel are available, *but the effective development of the world* in order to put an end to hunger and disease, it must be framed in different terms. Here private initiative and the purely capitalist systems as they exist in a derived form at the present day are both powerless, as are the governments of the developed countries, if they do not revise their ideas.

When capitalism takes a hand in development, it is not concerned with *authentic* development; nor is this, indeed, its true function. Its role is to utilize certain resources in order to place products on the market, and in doing this to ensure the highest possible profit for the enterprises themselves and the maximum dividends for the shareholders.

Consequently, capitalism tends towards what is profitable rather than towards what is strictly necessary. And in the view of capitalism necessary things are those which are needed by the rich countries, not those which are vitally necessary for the countries where the resources are to be found.

Capitalism, whether intentionally or not, can produce a certain kind of dynamic economic balance within a highly-developed capitalist country, adapting itself to crises haphazardly as they arise. This balance indeed is not its primary concern; it operates only insofar as it ensures the continuation of capitalist profits.

A typical case concerns the royalties from oil. The exploitation of oil deposits today is usually, where powerful companies have been formed for that purpose, an operation with a high profit margin. In fact, 70 per cent of the capital invested abroad during the five years after the Second World War were in oilfields. That the Suez affair or a break in the pipelines can have such a detrimental effect on these profits, arises from the very nature of the companies themselves.

The fact that profits from oil may be extravagant, or unwisely spent, is of little concern to the oil companies, unless it threatens to reduce their yields and profits in any way.

It is estimated that in 1955 the revenue from the oilfields and the amount of money spent on the spot by the oil companies represented about 10 per cent of the total income of Iran and Syria, 33 per cent that of Iraq, between 45 and 60 per cent that of Bahrein and Saudi Arabia, and more than 90 per cent in the case of Kuwait and Katar. The amount of money paid directly to the governments of the Middle Eastern countries rose to about $500 million in 1953 and $680 million in 1954, as against $200 million in 1950. Between 1950 and 1955, the income directly derived from the exploitation of the oil fields and allotted to the governments concerned rose by 340 per cent. During the same period, the total amount of crude oil produced rose by 83 per cent.

These figures are amazing. Iraq, at least, in spite of allowing a certain amount of waste, has carefully used some of this income to reclaim land through irrigation and has "put the money to work." But in Saudi Arabia, a country where slavery is still legal, it has had hardly any effect except that of greatly increasing the king's colossal wealth and expenditure. And in Kuwait, a largely desert and almost uninhabited country lacking any potential resources other than oil, there is a clear need for the development that could be undertaken with the enormous sum of 200 million dollars paid every year for the rent of its oilfields.

GROWTH CONTRASTED WITH DEVELOPMENT

In his *Réflexions sur l'économie de l'Afrique Noire,* Mamadou Dia described the erratic but normal progress of economic growth which fails to produce an objectively sound development of resources.

We know the nature of the progress of this evolution which is characteristic of the evolution of capitalism in previously subject countries. Preoccupied with the search for outlets for its manufactured products, investing only surplus capital and not any worthwhile proportion of the capital available, and anxious only to ensure that it will continue to be able to exploit raw materials, imperialistic capitalism assumes an aspect which distinguishes it from that of countries which have an autonomous economy. One of its most pronounced tendencies is to turn its back on every attempt at industrialization made on African soil. This attitude corresponds perfectly with its chief aim, which is to reserve these territories as outlets for the industries of the European "mother" countries. The chief emphasis, one might say the exclusive emphasis, is put on the production of raw material destined either to feed the industrial maws of the dominant economies, or to supply the dominant economies with whatever agricultural products they do not produce themselves.

The capital funds which, during this period of free enterprise, are almost exclusively private, are invested (and this is a natural consequence of the system) in the sectors of the economy where all the benefits are already earmarked for the dominant economy and particularly for the special interests of non-African shareholders in enterprises concerned with agriculture, export and inevitably mining. Where agriculture is concerned, we witness the neglect of essential food crops and the concentration on industrial crops such as coffee, cotton, ground-nuts, and castor-oil plants, to name the main if not the only ones. In this way, the peasant subsistence economy gives way to a capitalist economy which lacks the intelligence to integrate Africa into the modern world, and rather chooses to remain a trading economy whose only concern is to encourage the accumulation of capital and the growth of dividends to the greatest possible extent.

The consequences of this kind of system are obvious. From any point of view, they are most serious. It is this system which is responsible for the sclerosis which is affecting African agriculture, for the deficiency of the soil which has now become particularly alarming, for the progress of erosion and the constant encroachment of the desert. All these evils could have been avoided by the rationalization of the system of growing crops for export and the modernization of the peasant economy. It is true that this presupposes, on the part of colonial capitalism, an unlikely conversion to the idea of improving the lot of the native thanks to scientific progress. On the contrary, however, by virtue of its passion to accumulate high profits, a capitalist economy, as well as striking a serious blow at the resources of the land, strikes an equally serious blow at the human resources of a country through the imbalance created between industrial and essential food crops, and through the undernourishment which is its result. How can we continue to wonder at the low productivity of the black laborer, whose production is destined principally for export, and in return for which his country will receive manufactured articles whose virtues do not include those of strengthening the body?[1]

Some people may say that these are exaggerations, and represent a Marxist interpretation. Perhaps so, to a certain extent. But parallel passages can be found in the documents published by the United Nations Organization.

The most generous attempts in principle to solve the problem always involve to some extent the desire for a profit which will sustain capitalist enterprises.

The world's responsibility is even greater, when it comes to the world arms race, which was soundly denounced by Gunnar Myrdal over a decade ago:

The huge present-day effort for rearmament has considerably reinforced the long-established tendency to weight investment in favor of the already industrialized countries. The expenditure on national defense in the principal industrial countries of Western and Eastern Europe, in the Soviet Union and in the United States, will soon increase to the point where the total sum so spent will be equal, if not even greater than, the total amount of the national incomes of all the insufficiently developed countries taken together, and will be about 20 times greater than the total

[1] Mamadou Dia, *Reflexions sur l'economie de l'Afrique Noire* (Paris: Editions Africaines, 1952), pp. 27–30.

amount invested in the national reserve funds of these countries.[2]

The capitalist system, by providing communism with its *raison d'être* and an opportunity to oppose it, and through its failure to show at its outset that it had sufficient human qualities to benefit a large number of people, has, apart from the incapacity of its internal logic to organize the world on behalf of the common good, introduced a dialectic of conflict which exhausts the entire world—East and West—in gigantic military efforts. Capitalism can control a massive capacity for surplus production in order to wage war or prepare for war. Why should not this great potential be harnessed to ensure the development of the underdeveloped countries and for the collective good of humanity? It is because such a policy cannot be combined with profit-making. The essential motive force of capitalism therefore can only be profit.

The only salvation for capitalism is that it should accept, and even pursue, the various forms of voluntary altruism imposed by clear-sighted national and international legislation, imposing on itself the discipline and self-sacrifice which would place it, as a whole, at the service of the international common good.

[2] Gunnar Myrdal, "Les Aspects économiques de la santé," *op. cit.*, p. 795.

13

Paternalistic, Insufficient and Unadapted Aid

*Hesitant and tardy acts of generosity on the part
of the advanced countries tend less to develop
the countries to which they are directed than to
put them under an obligation.*

The law of profit prevents the massive investment of private
capital in the underdeveloped countries. The inadequacy
or the complete lack of a basic economic framework, and
the prevailing political uncertainty, discourage foreign capital. The figures for private investments show a decrease
(6.2 billion dollars in 1962 compared with 6.4 in 1961). The
only course of action left to the backward countries is that
of turning to their own reserves, private or state-levied, or
to national and international public assistance.

THE LATIN AMERICAN COUNTRIES

The rate of total investment in certain already industrialized Latin American countries, in relation to the national
income, is on the order of 14 per cent. It is therefore not
far removed from the investment rate of the developed
countries. But actual resources available for investment are

much smaller, because the national income per inhabitant is one-third that of European developed countries and one-seventh or one-eighth that of the United States.

Investment is turning more and more towards the industries which promise a high profit rather than to those which are objectively the most necessary. In countries where development is still in its infancy, speculative profit is still greater than industrial profit. For this reason, speculation on crop-growing or stock-raising, on building sites, and on apartments reaches such incredible proportions.

It has been calculated that the construction of all the buildings in Sao Paulo on the total area of land which has already been divided up would correspond, with regard to the density with which the built-up part is inhabited at the moment, to a population of some 22 million. Some 33 square miles of the land stretching along the Praia Grande, to the southwest of Santos, can already be considered as having been divided up or bought for speculative purposes.

Wherever a road is to be built, adjoining land passes from one buyer to another at escalating profits of anything from 50 to 1,000 per cent. The colossal fortunes to be made in this way attract an important part of the national reserves away from productive investment.

Furthermore, many people with money at their disposal attempt to provide against any possible depreciation by buying American dollars or securities. The amount of capital leaving the country is therefore considerable.

Governments consequently find themselves hard put to establish the basic economic requirements of roads, railways, canals, ports, airports, power stations, schools, and hospitals. And insofar as private industry is not interested in them, the government has to see to the provision and creation of basic industries such as mines, steel works and petroleum refineries. They are frequently forced to look abroad and to the international organizations for help.

THE EUROPEAN EFFORT IN BLACK AFRICA

The situation is evidently more difficult in the world's least developed countries. Here the total level of state-levied reserves amounts to perhaps as little as 5 per cent of the national income, an income sometimes one-tenth that in European countries per inhabitant and one-thirtieth that in the United States. Those countries which receive, thanks to their petroleum or mineral resources, high royalties, can still plan a significant development and exploitation program. Other countries which do not receive gifts or significant loans, are condemned to underdevelopment.

The European mother countries have, since 1945, begun to understand this situation, particularly in relation to Black Africa, and have accomplished a considerable amount.

Taking into account private, semi-public and public investment not included in specific plans of development, this represents nearly 7.5 billion dollars for investment, that is, an annual figure of about 750 million dollars. When set beside the number of inhabitants (more than 100 million) this figure represents an effort at least as important as that undertaken by the United States on behalf of the countries which are dependent on it. We should also recognize, in the meantime, that Marshall Plan aid has had by no means a negligible effect on the development of the African countries.

France, through the medium of organizations such as the F.I.D.E.S. (Investment Funds for Overseas Development) and F.I.D.O.M. (Special Funds for the French Overseas Provinces through the Monnet Plan), and in other ways has effectively assisted Black Africa to the extent of 1 billion dollars in ten years.

THE COLOMBO PLAN

We must also underline the importance of the help given to certain Far Eastern countries through Britain's initiative and the Colombo Plan. This plan is concerned with the following countries: Burma, Cambodia, Ceylon, India, Indonesia, Laos, Malaysia, British Borneo, Nepal, Pakistan, the Philippines, Thailand, and Vietnam.

Different reports of the Colombo Plan, started among Commonwealth countries of Southeast Asia in 1950, have been able to state that a notable increase in national income has taken place in several countries in this area, and that in a number of them this increase has outstripped the rise in population.

The accompanying table shows the amount of participation in the Colombo Plan from July 1, 1951 to June 30, 1958 by the United Kingdom, Australia, Canada, New Zealand, and Japan.

These subsidies are allotted in their entirety to mutually agreed projects decided on by the donor and recipient governments.

	Million dollars
United Kingdom	345
Canada	130
Australia	61
New Zealand	20
Japan	0.7
	556.7

The I.B.R.D. (International Bank for Reconstruction and Development) lent 816 million dollars between 1951 and 1958. The government of the United States, during the same period, supplied 4 billion dollars, some of which took the form of loans repayable in local currency.

AMERICAN AND I.B.R.D. FINANCIAL AID

It would be invidious not to recognize the importance of American financial aid abroad. From July 1, 1946, through June 30, 1963, United States foreign aid consisted approximately of 90 billion dollars. Of this amount, about 32.1 billion dollars were used for military supplies and services; 57.4 billion dollars were used for economic as well as technical assistance.

In 1962 foreign aid reached a total of over 5 billion dollars: 2.8 billion in loans and 2.2 in gifts.

Various organizations act as intermediaries in the disbursement of these sums. The E.C.A. (Economic Cooperation Administration) and the M.S.A. (Mutual Security Agency) gave 330 million dollars to Southeast Asia for technical assistance between 1950 and 1952. Both military and economic aid is supplied by the M.S.A.

Credits afforded to the underdeveloped regions by the United States Export-Import Bank amounted to 569 million dollars in 1958–1959, compared with 452 million dollars in 1957–1958. As well as loans from individual countries, we must take into account those from the International Bank for Reconstruction and Development (I.B.R.D.): 659 million dollars for the period 1959–1960, 610 million for 1960–1961. These are, of course, international loans, but the share of the United States is by far the greatest.

On the suggestion of the United States and in order to avoid the danger of the various donor countries trying to outbid one another, an affiliate of the I.B.R.D., the International Development Association (I.D.A.), was created in 1960. This body is responsible for the distribution of credits.

Agriculture, unfortunately, has not figured largely either in the credits of the Export-Import Bank or in the I.B.R.D. Moreover, a large part of the economic aid supplied bilaterally was actually for "defense purposes" (one-third of the total for the year 1959).

TECHNICAL ASSISTANCE IS TOO MEAGER

If gifts and loans constitute one aspect of aid to the underdeveloped countries, we must not forget that technical assistance plays a primary role, even though its cost may form only a small fraction of the total aid expenditure.

As many nations still have, in some sense, overseas territories which are dependent on them or associated with them, they have in each of these countries an important number of assistants and experts. Some of these will be there on a permanent basis, others will have been sent out for a few years on a tour of duty.

Technical assistance has a wide sphere of application: communications, railways, mines, power stations, canals, irrigation, drainage, navigation, ports and their hinterland, airports, basic industries, processing industries, banks, insurance, public administration, urbanization, regional government, statistics, coordination and planning. To these we must add agronomy, technology, veterinary and sanitary assistance, and instruction and education in all its forms. We can see therefore the importance of the role which can be fulfilled by peripatetic advisers who visit villages or groups of villages.

Even on a regional or national scale the services of experts on coordination—who are still unfortunately few in number—appear to be necessary.

This incomplete list is enough to give some idea of the total number of foreign personnel necessary for the adequate exploitation of the resources of the underdeveloped part of the world. We must realize that technical assistance is still a comparatively recent development. In the course of a recent international conference on the question of technical cooperation, it was emphasized that a target of one million experts would be required by 1970, compared with one hundred thousand (45 thousand of whom were French) in 1962. It must also be said that assistants and experts vary considerably in quality. If there are many remarkably good ones, there are sometimes others who, by their lack of tact, bring technical assistance into disrepute, perhaps through lack of experience of the country in which they are working, or perhaps through a lack of adaptability, or even through a streak of Western arrogance. The assistant or expert must know how to divest himself of the trappings of his own civilization, so that he may be able to understand the civilization in which he has become involved and that he may be able to appreciate its authentic values.

BALANCE-SHEET: PATERNALISM AND A LACK OF ADAPTABILITY

What conclusions can be drawn from all these facts?

At first, perhaps, there is a temptation to yield to a feeling of satisfaction. The selfishness of the wealthy nations seems, in effect, to have been broken down.

When we look at the facts more closely, however, we see that the problem of aid has not been solved by these still tardy and still hesitant acts of kindness.

We have seen the equivocal nature of American aid, where direct or indirect military aid is much greater than economic aid, and where even economic aid is largely determined by political or military considerations. Countries which are being assisted or which want to be assisted have not been slow to perceive this, and several have skillfully made a bargaining point of the possibility of a plea for aid to the U.S.S.R. The problem has changed from one of fraternal assistance with an eye to harmonized and integral development, and has become a problem of searching for a defense bulwark.

From now on competition between the U.S. and the U.S.S.R. in giving aid to the underdeveloped countries is out in the open. Everybody is aware of the important Soviet contribution to the Aswan Dam in Upper Egypt. Until now

90 per cent of the credits have been allocated to a small number of countries: the U.A.R., Iraq, Afghanistan, India, and Indonesia. But contacts have been made with many others: Turkey, Yemen, Burma, Cambodia, and Ceylon.

The U.S.S.R. allots its loans on a long-term basis and at very low rates of interest. It accepts payment in kind (cotton in the case of Egypt, for example) for which it is sometimes difficult to find a market.

At the beginning of 1959 it was estimated that the Soviet bloc had accorded some 2.4 billion dollars worth of gifts and credits to the underdeveloped non-Communist countries. Russia furthermore greatly enlarged her sphere of influence by sending out scientific teams.

In the face of this competition, American aid risks losing whatever semblance of disinterested generosity it can still command. President Eisenhower's message on January 9, 1958, is still characteristic of America's state of mind. This speech on peace began by formulating the first imperative: the safeguarding of America, which was menaced principally by Communist imperialism. The United States has spent over 400 billion dollars since Korea on maintaining and reinforcing its defense forces. Today's problem is to increase the amount of foreign aid in order to allow the countries assisted to turn against Communism and increase their trade. It is far from ideal when one has to prove that one is acting from a sincere love of humanity.

The Colombo Plan is certainly an aid plan, but it is clear that its object is to maintain, if not to extend, Britain's political influence and to preserve a market for her goods. It has also provided Britain with the opportunity to profit from the French disaster in Indochina.

The effort displayed by the European colonial countries in Black Africa—without question the greatest such effort in favor of the underdeveloped countries—shows an overwhelming desire to compensate for the resentment they had formerly aroused and to resist American influence.

If we leave aside the political aspect and only examine the economic side of things, it must be stated quite categorically that the world total of aid to the underdeveloped countries is inadequate when it is placed against their needs. As François Perroux remarks:

Development projects, even where they are not jeopardized by rearmament, do not exist on the required scale. . . . Plans are neither set out nor strictly coordinated. We still have an English plan and an American plan. Everything is done as if the old doctrine of "spheres of influence" were still the foundation of all activity, as if the dominant economy of the nineteenth century and that of the twentieth were prolonging selfish competition in humanitarian and political work. The privileged nations show that they have been transformed, converted somewhat perhaps, but still retaining their mental reservations or ivory towers. The common attitude of white men towards black men is not yet that of a crusade whose sole intention is the preservation of life, the promotion of social and economic growth and the making of reparation for past exactions and unfair exploitation.[2]

The Americans do not suspect how unpleasant the parading of their generosity appears. In 1962 their foreign aid amounted to more than 5 billion dollars. This is a great deal undoubtedly; it is certainly much more than in previous

[2] François Perroux, *L'Europe sans rivages* (Paris: Presses Universitaires de France, 1954), p. 407.

years, but it is still too little. Even if we take the very low estimates which were drawn up some years ago, and which allowed for the low intake capacity of the underdeveloped countries, the developed countries should devote a minimum of 10 billion dollars annually to the underdeveloped countries as a whole. In 1957 they allotted 3 billion for this purpose, and 8.7 in 1961. This is still far below the necessary level.

The United States is still the largest provider in terms of actual cash; but if we take its contribution in proportion to its total national production, it is less than that of the French: 0.9 per cent of the national output as against 2.9 per cent in 1962.

In 1963, according to Reginald Maudling, Great Britain contributed 200 million pounds in aid, to which should be added 150 million pounds from private investments and 25 million pounds in military aid. This adds up to a total representing 1.25 per cent of its gross national product.

It is not necessary, of course, that financial aid from the rich countries should be fixed in arithmetical proportion to the national income. Nor need it be fixed so that it is proportionate to the excess revenue per inhabitant in relation to the maximum level of development—400 dollars, for example. It should, however, be progressive according as the levels become higher. In a country where there was an excess of 200 dollars per inhabitant, for example, it should be normal that the country should endeavor to contribute between 2 and 5 per cent of this surplus, and a country with a surplus of 1,000 dollars would contribute 10 per cent, if not more. Countries levy a sliding taxation scale on incomes above a certain level in order to solve their domestic financial problems. The principle is no less valid for the solution of world problems involving the human race which is acquiring more and more solidarity, and can no longer afford to ignore the question of overall development.

However, the objective proposed by experts is a modest one, and amounts to an increase of 2 per cent in the incomes of the underdeveloped countries. An increase of 2 per cent in the national income of the United States would represent a substantial increase amounting to about 400 dollars in the income of every American. In countries where the national income is between 40 and 100 dollars, it would mean a rise of between 80 cents and 2 dollars. And even this would not prevent the gap from widening inexorably as time goes on. The present-day relationship between the standard of living of the undeveloped and that of the highly developed countries, which is in the region of 1 to 50, would increase by the end of the century to at least 1 to 100. A completely optimistic calculation shows that the rate of increase in the living standards of the poor peoples would have to be at least twice that experienced by the wealthy nations.

If Canada devotes 1/1000 of her national income to the Colombo Plan, this is a good thing. But it should not be enough to reassure Canadian consciences.

François Perroux was right to denounce virulently the greatest sin of our era as "national greed."

14

The Disintegration of Civilizations
and the Revolt against the West

*In Western schools, children are taught how
to earn money. In Burmese monasteries, they
are taught how to lead a happy and contented
life.*

—Alexander D. Peterson[1]

DISINTEGRATION OF CIVILIZATIONS

The Evidence of Travellers

There are several symptomatic facts which have to be explained if we are to understand the problem of the fragmentation of civilizations. These facts can be drawn from Algeria and Black Africa.

About 200,000 nomads live in Algeria by raising cattle. The pasture lands there do not bear the slightest resemblance to those of Europe. Depending on whether there is any rain, a few blades of grass may appear for every acre in one tiny, unpredictable area.

Several years ago, when one asked a tribal chief what he

[1] Alexander D. Peterson, *The Far East* (Chester Springs, Pa.: Dufour, 1957).

wanted, he would reply: "I do not want anything. I have butter, milk and wool, and the pastures are good." The white administrators made their rounds on horseback; they would meet the local chiefs and sleep out under canvas. Their wives were happy with this sort of life, continually moving around, and living in tents, however hard it was, and many were even proud of it.

On the eve of Algerian independence the administrator used to set out in a jeep for the day only; and his wife remained behind secure in the knowledge that he would return the same evening. Thus contact between the native populations and the French officials was lost.

The local chief established his seat in a town, and left the herd to be looked after by hired men. The women were glad of this, because it meant that they had less work to do and were able to meet each other more easily.

In this fashion the nomad way of life was seriously threatened. Certain responsible white men think that it should be completely abandoned. What was the use of finding water holes and training shepherds? What had been condemned had been condemned. Others thought that the best solution was to create "reserves." No one believes now that any effort should have been made to save the remnants of an uprooted past.

The most important groups of pygmies were, without doubt, those found in what was formerly the Belgian Congo. The young King of the Belgians, seeing their living conditions, asked that something should be done for them. But what was there to be done? Some well-meaning administrator would doubtless have built better huts for them nearer the roads, thinking that he would in this way have improved their condition. The result would have been the exact opposite. These hunters needed the forest, and needed to live there in proximity to their quarry, moving around at random or according to the way that the game was moving. Fixing them in one place would not necessarily turn them into farmers, and the negro villagers, who already exploited the pygmies and held them in a strictly dependent state amounting almost to slavery, would have either dominated them even more or would have upbraided them for ceasing to provide them with game.

The bushmen, who are even more primitive, were in no more favorable a position.

Throughout Black Africa can be seen the effects of the oversimplified idea of progress which haunts the spirit of the white race. Complete, isolated houses were built, while their designers neglected the traditional courtyard around which an enlarged family lived in hierarchical units, forming the essential unit of the civilization. By bringing doubtful comfort, the social structure was shattered.

In the black quarters surrounding the small residential oases of Frenchmen or Syrio-Lebanese can be seen a subproletarian population torn away from its traditions in spite of the tremendous number of relatives who cluster around anyone who has found a job.

We are also aware of the destruction, in human terms, wreaked on the black workers who come from many tribes and pass through the mines. The amount of intoxicants they consume on their free days is frightening.

In the other part of the world, the white man has not been cruel to the Hawaiians. Nevertheless, their numbers have been decimated in less than a century.

It is also admitted that in South America the Amazon Indian tribes do not possess a high degree of resistance to contact with more advanced peoples. The illnesses whose germs are carried by Europeans attack the non-immunized tribes with particular virulence.

The first impression received by the traveller overseas is that our civilization appears to be one which destroys values. This superficial impression is unfortunately confirmed by analyses made by ethnologists, sociologists and economists.

The Evidence of Experts

United Nations experts have examined the social upheavals produced by the introduction of industrialization in the underdeveloped countries. They have noted the radical change in the way of life which this has produced. They have commented on the powerlessness of societies to solve the enormous problems of adaptation which are inherent in a more or less radical modification of a country's social and economic structure.

The following remarks are based on a UN study of the tensions specifically due to industrialization:[2]

Specialization and mass production dislocate the original family-based system of production, breaking up the framework within which the worker could find a relatively assured security.

Commercialization and the utilization of money tend to break down systems of mutual assistance and communal

[2] UN, *Processes and Problems of Industrialization in Under-Developed Countries* (December, 1954).

cooperation; competition and individualism break the village spirit, leaving the individual without protection and without a scale of values which he can substitute for the old ones.

Thus the village customs (feats of strength or skill, traditional ceremonies and so on) which colored his life and prevented him from feeling poor and disinherited, all disappear.

The disappearance of the craftsman class and also the disappearance of special distinguishing qualities (such as hereditary wealth, in some groups) increase the tension.

The exodus towards the towns which is accelerated by the rapid growth of the rural population also tears men away from the normal framework of their social life.

To these must be added the degrading conditions which accompany life in the shanty towns, the low standards of health which are created as a result, the overcrowded accommodation, delinquency, crime, exploitation of the workers, and so on.

Very often when such a town springs up, it will produce a disproportion between the relative numbers of members of either sex, accentuating the consequences of a departure from the normal mode of family life. The traditional form of family life is fractured and with it all the human richness which it enshrined.

The emancipation of women is another consequence of factory work. The family unit in urban life is represented by the couple, no longer by the patriarchal group.

It is often tempting to try to transpose the social legislation of the developed countries in an effort to remedy social evils in the underdeveloped countries. But in fact these laws are inapplicable, either for financial reasons because productivity is not high enough, or because the working class has no trade-union tradition and is not adapted to such laws.

The fragmentation of the original communities raises the question of the creation of a new form of "social security" based on the community as a whole. But there is an inevitable hiatus between these two forms of protection, and governments have to be careful not to outrun their financial capability if they do not want to jeopardize long-term development.

Georges Balandier, a very competent authority on Africa, wrote several extremely lucid pages in *Le Tiers Monde* about the social price that has to be paid for progress.[3] Economic progress imposes a whole series of chain-reaction upheavals which affect the material structure of traditional societies as well as their intangible elements. It demands a changed distribution of land, considerable population movement, a new professional structure, and harder and more concentrated work in order to produce results which are often very slow in being realized. These changes provoke discontent and tension; and this is why so many new governments have to find foreign scapegoats whom they can hold responsible and on to whose shoulders they can transfer the resentment of their people.

Balandier believes that the exodus from the country to the rapidly spreading towns will double in a few years, with definite effects on the national economy. These towns are surrounded by shack and shanty towns where the migrant population piles up in ever-increasing numbers. Speculation in land, houses, and rents makes heavy demands on wages that are in general the lowest possible in the circumstances. The

[3] *Le Tiers Monde, op. cit.* pp. 300–303.

new arrivals cannot all find jobs. The town's food supply does not keep pace with its growth.

Men attracted to the towns by the hope of work are not followed until later by a smaller number of women. Prostitution is intensified, with consequent drastic modifications to the familial structure. Conflicts arise between different groups in the inorganic, growing city; the crime rate increases both among adults and young people; the unstable, ill-equipped and badly-paid proletariat does not possess the means to ensure that it gets its rights; and social degradation follows.

Since 1945, however, a crisis of conscience has taken place and a genuinely humanistic impulse has been felt throughout the world. The foundation of FAO and WHO, the Declaration of Human Rights, the Truman doctrine of "Point IV," and where Africa is concerned, the tardy but important effort made by the European colonial powers, have all been indications of this. But nevertheless, according as censuses and inquiries have revealed with increasing clarity the numerical increase of the population in the underdeveloped countries and the extent of their minimum needs, and as the ingratitude displayed by the assisted countries produces more resentment, and as the opposition between West and East intensifies, so have the "petit bourgeois" calculations of the privileged nations been given priority.

Why, for example, should one make sacrifices in order to assist the hungry peoples to increase and multiply? We do not recognize our responsibility for this increase. Did not the hygienic and sanitary measures taken in the underdeveloped countries reduce the infant mortality and the overall mortality rate? A position embodying the defense of life had therefore been adopted in regard to these peoples, forgetting, however, that it was necessary to apply oneself at the same time to the preservation of the soil, the irrigation of arable land, and the improvement of animal and vegetable strains.

A FALSE REMEDY: BIRTH CONTROL

And this is where the Western world took fright. The first objective, the great civilizing factor, became contraceptive propaganda. No heed was paid to the moral disasters which have occurred even in the West owing to "eugenic" practices. The essential remedy for the evils of humanity could be realized only through the voluntary limitation of births, abortion included.

We are aware of measures of this kind which were taken in Japan under American pressure. The birth rate fell from 34 per thousand in 1947 to 17 in 1961. In 1953 there had already been more than a million legal abortions. R. Guillain estimated that the total number of abortions in 1957 was 2,400,000, while there were in the same year only 1.5 million live births.

Advocates of birth control take up this position. The gap between figures for births and deaths (they say), which is increasing in many of the underdeveloped countries, forces one to ask whether it is possible to reduce fertility in these zones through a deliberate effort, rather than await the slow progress of social evolution or the horrifying possibility of a rise in the mortality rate. The way to persuade under-developed rural populations into adopting birth control techniques is fraught with difficulties. On the other hand, contraceptive methods in use in the developed societies can be adapted without very great expense to countries which are undeveloped or whose population, in relation to the country's total income, is too high. The cost could be as low as between 1 and 5 cents per family per week. The cost for public collective efforts, therefore, is low when compared to the world-wide cost of a development program.

Where acceptance of contraceptive methods is concerned, it seems that attitudes differ from one country to another. But studies of the subject are still few and far between. Some authors, nevertheless, are "optimistic" or "full of hope" about this subject. Some governments are adopting the attitude that they will initiate a deliberate program in spite of idealistic or religious objections.

However, the intervention of the advanced countries to ensure the execution of a large-scale plan for the reduction of fertility can be undertaken only with extreme delicacy. Louis Henry has explained how contraceptive propaganda, fostered by outside influence, can arouse opposition among the population.

Intemperate birth control propaganda inspired by the West could eventually produce a collective unfavorable reaction and a result diametrically opposite to the one intended. This is even more likely if, as the cultural context is different, such an action runs the risk of being interpreted as an indirect attempt to weaken a non-Western culture.[4]

But this objection appears irrelevant when it happens that the intellectuals of the underdeveloped countries endorse the birth control campaign. For Professor Chandrasekhar, world demographic policy must include the world-wide use of

[4] *Ibid.*, p. 173.

contraceptive practices. According to him, "no well-conceived world demographic policy could be either complete or effective without the universal knowledge and application of contraceptive methods." The West, therefore, can register with satisfaction its greatest victory since the end of the Second World War. Having taught people how to destroy or prevent life, it may be shocked at some future date when invading forces refuse to respect the value which Western people place on their own lives.

When the human conscience has become accustomed to a certain crime, this brings about a general deterioration and threatens respect for the life of the individual. Programs of contraception are among the most important items on the balance sheet of Western action on behalf of the under-developed countries.

FROM DISINTEGRATION TO REVOLT

The terms "disintegration" and "fragmentation" when applied to the non-European civilizations are not, therefore, too harsh. The advanced Western world has, through its technical superiority and practical materialism, dislocated centuries-old traditions, provoked envy, and paved the way for revolt.

Georges Balandier analyzed it like this.

The multiple and rapid displacement of populations, the ever-increasing tempo of world economy, and the heightened effectiveness of the communications media, including press, radio and cinema, have breached the most distant socio-cultural frontiers. The example set by the industrial nations with a high standard of living forces itself on people who are living on the periphery of this influence, and suggests a way of life which they could not have even imagined a century or less ago. Poverty is old, but the discovery that there are remedies for it is of recent origin.[5]

J. Mallet explains the transition to revolt in this way.

It seems that Western civilization's effectiveness, which is demonstrated practically every day, has given the West a type of superiority complex. This prevents it from envisaging any form of progress other than that which involves the promulgation of its own standards of value. But this does not even begin to justify the racial privileges which the European minorities overseas have arrogated to themselves.

In the first phase, a sense of gratitude prevails over resentment among the colonized peoples. Abuses and injustice will not, at this stage, have provoked any rebellion by the masses, who are amazed to see despotism put to rights, and also the perversions of justice and of local government. They find in new creeds or in new modes of life a way to liberate themselves from the constraint of old customs—not all of them very respectable—of superstition and of the former social groupings. For the masses it represents a provisional freedom to work in the city, in the factories, or on European-sponsored projects.

[But during a second phase] the irruption of the modern world and its techniques completely upsets the social structure of the colonies, which rapidly disintegrates under the shock of an unprecedented revolution which, in a few years, brings it into the age of electricity and the airplane. A great gap is left by the disappearance of the ancient beliefs, and it is a gap that Christianity does not seem able to fill. The growing cities house a disorientated, wretched proletariat. At the same time, the

[5] *Ibid.*, p. 122.

increase in the standard of living and the development of education both contribute to the creation of a prosperous class of townsmen, merchants and landowners, and multiply the number of people who have "evolved" along Western lines. These suffer because they are not allowed to assume responsibility, and are rejected by the European society to which they would have liked to attach themselves.[6]

The sequel is well-known. It involves a progressive revolt whose strength of purpose was expressed at Bandung with such unforeseeable intensity and scope. It can be seen in the attempt to reestablish Arab unity, in the agitation of the countries under foreign domination or tutelage who demand their independence. It can be seen in the United Nations, making its powerlessness obvious. It can be seen in Russian–American competition to provide arms, iron foundries or dams. It can be seen in the fact that civilization everywhere is threatened.

The reaction of the underdeveloped countries against those countries which were formerly the pivotal areas of the world has assumed such immense proportions that it has practically swamped the great colonial empires. But it is also true that reaction against American economic domination is already both considerable and noticeable. This is the reason for Mamadou Dia's writing as follows:

Contrary to the objectives laid down by Point IV, American capital is invested, not in the peasant farming countries, but almost exclusively in the countries where the nature of the subsoil permits the extraction of minerals, such as copper in Rhodesia, tin in the Congo, manganese in the Gold Coast, gold

[6] *Ibid.*, pp. 37, 40.

ore in Liberia and Sierra Leone, and finally, diamonds, cobalt and colombite in Central Africa. This tendency would directly result in a form of colonialism that, if it is not vigorously resisted, would be even more lethal than that which the Americans claim to have been fighting since the beginning of the century. Some African states, whose leaders have adopted an attitude of thinly disguised hostility towards the United States, have realized this. Mr. Nkrumah, Prime Minister of Ghana, is one. He has studied in the United States; but this has not lessened his aversion to the dollar.[7]

For the Negro writer who formulated that warning, the change-over from the colonial pact to an economy depending on inadequate and badly distributed gifts, will not minimize the aggressiveness of those who were formerly dominated or otherwise exploited.

If the Western world attracts the attention of the colonial peoples, it is rather because of the pressure which its overt culture exercises on their old social and economic structures. . . . they see the Western regime of money and everything that money represents taking precedence over their traditional economy. They see the economic transformations modifying their social system, and, for example, replacing the old system of family ownership by the ownership of property by individuals or by the letting of land. Africans today see their old world overrun; and, as the old world disappears, a new one must take its place. On what foundation is it to be built?[8]

This is the question which we must now examine.

[7] *Réflexions sur l'économie de l'Afrique Noire, op. cit.*, pp. 38–39.
[8] UN, *Special Study on Social Conditions: Non-Self-Governing Territories* (April, 1953).

15

A Summing Up

There are many reasons for the reluctance of the more advanced and consequently richer peoples to take an objective view of the world situation.

The main reason is a certain kind of greed, that is, an immoderate love of possession. The former colonial powers were often steeped in this vice, and never succeeded in freeing themselves from it. But the new major powers are also possessed by the same vice in an even more virulent form.

In this context, the people and policies of the West are taking steps that will lead them to a repetition of the past. Instead of meeting a difficult situation fairly and squarely, and instead of recognizing the fact that mankind will be incapable of solving its problems if it does not rise above itself, they continue to take the short-sighted view in which nothing counts but the consolidation and the enlargement of their present state of well-being.

Obsessed by an intense desire to increase their possessions, they are afraid of making an honest evaluation of the blemishes in their own civilization. They cling desperately to the economic system which has made them rich, while they cut themselves off from the confidence and friendship of the underdeveloped peoples of the world.

They continue to preserve trading conditions characteristic of an economy run by shop-keepers, and maintain investment rules whose only basis is the calculation of profit. The suggestion that it is necessary to examine such conditions and to give satisfaction to human needs would seem to them to be naïve, as well as unintelligent and insupportable.

They have already increased the superiority of their standard of living by three, five, ten times as much as the rest of the world, which is often at a standstill if it is not in a decline. They consider it logical and just that the disparity between their standards of living will be at least doubled by the end of the century.

And nevertheless, belatedly and in direct contradiction to the system of which they boast, we see them timidly holding out mere handfuls of aid which, if increased, could give new hope to those who are deprived.

The grants that the richest among them would have you believe are enormous are in fact very slight, ineffective, and usually given from some ulterior motive. Such grants are only a sop to their dulled consciences. They bear no relation to the huge collective effort which would have to be undertaken to change effectively the lot of those who possess nothing.

These men do not see that their acts of generosity are insignificant, and that they would need to be increased at least tenfold, having regard to the surpluses of each individual nation on a world scale. To the poor they say: "Do as we do," without reflecting that this is impossible. Nor have they considered the lucid words of P. Rycmans about Black Africa: "Men are poor because they produce little; they produce little because they are too poor to provide themselves with the means to produce more."

The rich nations do not see that their commitment to the

hungry world is total. Their progress would become impossible were it not for the energy and raw materials with which these wretched people supply them. They evaluate the services rendered to them parsimoniously and in terms of an oppressive market.

They are surprised that they are neither loved nor understood while they destroy traditional institutions and values, and the fundamental ethical values of friendly human relations.

The Christian order of things is in fact closed to them, and the human order is, for them, only that of their own exaltation. The stupendous amount of thought and effort they expend on increasing their possessions blinds them to the right of all people, in a shrinking world and for the sake of a united human race, to at least the essentials of life. Their persistent greed has divorced them from the higher values of human living.

Part Five

Demands Made by a New Civilization:
TOWARD COORDINATED DEVELOPMENT

It is not a question of knowing whether
it is a good thing to encourage or
retard development, but of
understanding the conditions in which
development can take place and
making every effort to secure the best
possible form of evolution.
                                    —Alfred Sauvy

Those who in the West or in the East (Near and Far) are leaders in the political, economic, trade-union, intellectual, or spiritual fields, should no longer remain ignorant of the world situation, nor should they refuse to do anything to help in the solution of the world's present problems. Their laziness in not thinking about it, as well as their slackness when it comes to action, can only be criminal. When humanity is so gravely threatened, every shortcoming deserves punishment. Let us summarize the points expanded in our survey:

1. The earth will have more than 5 billion people by the year 2000.

2. Three-quarters of the human race is undernourished either

through lack of calories or through the lack of protective foods.

3. The primary problems for humanity therefore is this: There must be a considerable increase in food production to meet the need of those who are undernourished today and to provide for the increase in population.

4. The average income per person in the developed countries should increase by 36 per cent between 1962 and 1970. The corresponding figure for the less-developed countries for the same period will be only 9 per cent. The national income for the first group is now 14 times greater than that of the second. In 7 years it will be 17 times more. The difference in living standards is constantly growing.

5. Grants and loans from the wealthy countries are inadequate to ensure the necessary minimum for the entire human race.

6. The underdeveloped populations who are learning to read and are becoming aware of their plight, develop a growing reaction against the already developed countries. Now, as their demographic increase is very great, the relationship of power is changing continually in their favor.

7. Poverty and the awareness of poverty facilitate Communist infiltration in the underdeveloped countries of the non-collectivized part of the world.

8. Western rulers and thinkers do not seem to recognize the fact that the past is over and done with, and that a break must be made with obsolete theories and methods.

9. The world is becoming scientifically and technically one. The traditional civilizations are breaking up and there does not seem to be any new civilization emerging on a world scale.

To all this must be added the threat of self-destruction facing a world menaced by the existence of nuclear weapons.

In the face of these facts, several questions are particularly and urgently relevant:

How far can the underdeveloped countries ensure that their resources are adequately utilized?

What help can the advanced countries provide?

What kind of relationship should be established between countries which have reached different levels of development?

Is a new civilization practicable?

These are the questions which we must now try to answer.

16

Development Is Possible

*The human race must be examined nation by
nation, continent by continent; and while one
acknowledges that progress will be slow,
the methods which will make it possible and
ensure continuity have to be described.*

Experts have applied themselves to the essential problem of
development for several years: that is, is development possible? Their efforts have been, on the whole, both generous
and necessary. But whether their conclusions are optimistic
or pessimistic, they have in many cases tended to draw them
without taking sufficiently into account the differences which
are due to varying circumstances.

THREE TYPICAL CASES OF
DEVELOPMENT

It is quite certain that there are considerable opportunities
for improving the present situation. Three cases in particular
have impressed me in the course of my travels: the improvement of the Pontine Marshes in Italy, the "Hollambra"
fazenda between Campinas and Mogi-Mirim in the Brazilian

state of Sao Paulo, and the project at Fomeque in the Eastern Cordillera of the Colombian Andes.

The improvement of the Pontine area had not yet been completed. It involves, in effect, reclaiming a huge drowned basin and making land arable where previously the scourge of malaria made human habitation almost impossible. The control of the marshes, the digging or improvement of 1,240 miles of canals, the construction of almost 372 miles of roads, and the provision of an already important and extended irrigation system have nevertheless transformed an un-inhabited and almost totally unproductive area into a genuinely "humanized" and thickly populated one.

One plot of 72 acres which I visited had originally formed part of a large boggy area more or less covered by a lake. It can now support 85 head of prime cattle, and no food has to be brought in from outside. On this farm the "acclimatized" Dutch cows have an average yield of 3.5 gallons per day while they are in lactation, or more than 1,000 gallons a year. Beef cattle reach a weight of more than 10 cwts. in 16 months. The normal wheat yield is between 16 and 18 cwts. per acre, and the yield figure for sugar beet is between 100 and 140 or 160 cwts.

Many more comparable results could be quoted from other sectors of the Italian agrarian reform, which has been brought about by the provision of adequate economic foun-dations, and the experiments of agronomists and pilot farmers.

A very different type, and one which is even more reward-ing where results are concerned, is the "Hollambra" fazenda or cooperative in Brazil. This was founded in 1947 by a group of Dutch families on an area of some 12,500 acres of desolate countryside which had been abandoned largely to ill-conceived methods of farming and to the ants. The first attempt to develop the land involved half the total area and 100 families.

Economic success was prodigious. The Dutch cows took well to the land and their average yield turned out to be more than 2 gallons a day. Rotation of crops and sowings ensured that every day of the year trucks loaded with produce set off for Sao Paulo. The educational effort undertaken on behalf of the country's agricultural workers has been recently intensified. It is impossible to estimate the increase in the productive yield per acre. It is probably not an exaggeration to put it at 100 to 1.

The success experienced at Fomeque in Colombia is of another kind. Fomeque is a large mountain town between Bogota and the Orinoco plain which, in 20 years, has been completely transformed through the tenacious and intelligent initiative of a remarkable priest, Msgr. Gutierrez. His secret has been that he started by studying the inhabitants: their hopes, their needs, their troubles, and their capacity for enthusiasm. He pursued his study, family by family, and eventually came to the conclusion that he would have to promote not only their technical but their human and spiritual welfare at the same time, as well as their spirit of cooperation. His object was to arouse enthusiasm among the people for a great, practical project which would, in fact, come into existence.

Illiterate adults had to become well-taught farmers. Hidebound, lazy peasants had to be turned into farmers who could adapt their crops to the relief of the land, the quality of the soil, the climate, and the market. A conformist and more or less superstitious people had to become enlightened Christians.

From his very first meetings Msgr. Gutierrez, by keeping himself outside all existing parties, knew how to win the support of the leading men. From the beginning preoccupation with economic development was a never-abandoned theme. A cooperative society of peasants was formed to ensure economic development. A group of 6,000 shareholders provided 10,000 pesos in capital, which was used to buy a small plot of land for a pilot project.

This experimental "granja" showed how cattle, horses and farmyard animals could be improved in quality. When the peasants came to the center on Sundays, they were shown how it worked and technical advisers visited them in their homes.

The educational effort did not consist solely of multiplying the number of elementary schools for the children dispersed throughout the huge township. A literacy campaign was started from the beginning for adults and adolescents. Then a farm school was founded, followed by a school of sacred and folk music, a center for sport and physical culture, and catechetical centers.

A rural teachers' training college has already provided Colombia with some 200 teachers who come back in rotation every year and who follow a complementary correspondence course.

This is all backed up by a special course designed to improve the peasant's knowledge of farming techniques which is attended by people from as far away as Venezuela. In 1956 there were 87 pupils at a teachers' training college for foreign students. A school for training rural priests for village pastoral work has just been opened.

Thanks to this cultural and technical effort the area's economic life has developed rapidly. Yields have increased considerably. Selective farming has permitted the introduction of quality products, and tractors have been introduced. The cooperative now owns five trucks which collect the produce and sell it both collectively and directly. They also own a bulldozer.

Pupils in the upper classes in school have undertaken a campaign to improve the soil. This campaign aims at introducing contour ploughing, terracing and reforestation. Its purpose is to replace progressively up-and-down ploughing by horizontal cultivation.

In this way, the entire rural way of life has been transformed. Nearly all modern sports are practiced. Some 80 per cent of the houses have been improved. A hospital is being built. A workers' center has been constructed. As the domestic science schools also help to train nurses, there are many highly qualified people in charge of hygiene. Alcoholism has disappeared.

The earth therefore, if it is well treated, could certainly feed a world population 10 times its present size in the light of present-day technical knowledge, if the application of this knowledge were possible. But the draining and improvement of the Pontine marshes has cost Italy billions of lire; and the installation of one homestead at Hollambra meant that some 3 million francs had to be spent on equipment.

Fomeque, on the other hand, represents a progressive effort on the part of an impoverished population which was inspired, it is true, by an exceptional leader, and which through his action and example succeeded in communicating the communal spirit and sense of initiative. There a fourteen year old boy, for example, may already "own" a small piece of land or some livestock to prepare him for eventual responsibility. In this way new men are formed who are capable not only of improving their common lot, but of spreading their influence far and wide. The latest step in this project was taken when a contract was drawn up between the "co-operative" and the government providing for the development of 875,000 acres in the nearby province of Meta.[1]

THE DIFFICULTIES OF SUCCESS

We should not, however, on the basis of some successes which are infinitesimal in proportion to the total area of cultivated or cultivable land, leap to the conclusion that they can be general, or that the conditions necessary for success will obtain everywhere. Msgr. Gutierrez himself failed completely in the first attempt he made in another township. "The people," he says, "were not ready." We must guard against a number of naïve attitudes and mistakes which have gained currency among writers who specialize in these problems.

There is not a great deal of value in discussing the maximum possible number of people the world can feed and clothe. Men are localized, and in practice the great migratory movements are impossible which would distribute all the

[1] A comprehensive study of the economic, social and spiritual reforms needed in Latin America is contained in the work of François Houtart and Emile Pin, *The Church and the Latin American Revolution* (New York: Sheed and Ward, 1965).

land that still has to be won over to cultivation in an equitable way, or to be improved in such a way as to ensure that every area had the optimum population necessary to utilize its resources effectively and equalize living standards.

Alfred Sauvy has enumerated the many obstacles:

The difficulties which face the microscopically small migratory movements of the Reunion islanders to Madagascar or those of the Antilleans to Guiana are devastatingly relevant. And this is so in spite of the fact that the migratory movements are taking place between two areas under the same political jurisdiction. The population of India increases by between 3 and 4 million every year, that of Japan by more than a million. To re-direct even one-tenth of this surplus towards any country—which would, of necessity, have to be at quite a distance from the mother country—would require the expenditure of a great deal of money. The International Committee for European Migrations has estimated that it costs $13,000 to resettle one European family in America. Even if this figure were to be reduced by two-thirds, the resettlement of 250,000 Indian families overseas would cost $1 billion. And to what country would the emigrant ships take them?

No country considers welcoming masses of more or less destitute people who threaten to be unemployed or to work too hard; and to these difficulties must be added that of racial prejudice, whether it is admitted or not. In short, no country will think of providing a home for Indians, Egyptians or Japanese in appreciable numbers . . . This hallucinatory solution must therefore, except in exceptional cases, be abandoned.[2]

[2] Alfred Sauvy, *Théorie générale de la population*, 2 vols. (Paris: Presses Universitaires de France, 1952 and 1954), vol. II, pp. 209–210.

If we are to avoid being blinded by illusions, we have to start by taking a fresh look at our objectives. Western man has difficulty in realizing that his way of life is not the one common throughout the world. He has, as it were, canonized his scale of values and placed everything that tends towards success and happiness at its summit. When we communicate our ambition for these things to the people of different civilizations, we direct them towards idle fantasy, despair, and human disintegration.

Towards fantasy, in the first place, because to bring the whole world up to the Western standard of living is practically impossible not only in the next one or two generations, but doubtless even for the next few hundred years, assuming that large-scale wars are avoided and that the under-developed countries bring their rate of increase into line with that of the West.

Towards despair, in the second place, because the under-developed peoples, in attempting to achieve the impossible, will succeed only in being continually frustrated by their unsatisfied desires. By abandoning a humble scale of values which at the same time allowed them to believe that they were men, they dissipate themselves in pursuit of illusory values which are impossible of attainment.

In this way their collapse in human terms is assured.

TOWARD A GENUINE DEVELOPMENT

We can still distinguish between healthy, that is to say authentically humane, economic growth, and warped or anti-humane economic growth.

Growth expressed in terms of increased national income

per inhabitant can disguise an increase in the incomes of the rich and a corresponding impoverishment and regression in the incomes of the poor. In this case no development has taken place. Genuine development presupposes, in effect, an increase in the standard of living and in human standards which affects the huge, deprived mass of the population. It involves a generalized development of the whole human order, in every man and in all men.

The problem which humanity faces is that of achieving a concerted rise in standards unadulterated by the desire to omit necessary stages of development or to aim at spectacular and illusory progress. The problem is one of responding to the progressively greater need of each member of each country; a need not expressed in relation to a universal norm laid down by physical criteria alone, but in relation to the possibility of preserving and improving human values. It is without doubt a universal problem on a world-wide scale, but one which is diversified by men's concrete and limited hopes and by the variable natural conditions in which these are worked out.

To repeat it once more—discussions and suppositions about the needs of humanity *en bloc* are senseless. Each group of people has its roots in a certain part of the earth and must find its own formula for collective progress. If it uses Western values as its yardstick, the underdeveloped parts of the world can only lose their zeal for life and lapse into despair.

Wisdom, for the underdeveloped part of the world, lies in fighting misery while accepting poverty. It must strive for a certain level of economic growth, while refraining from its Western implications.

When we are speaking of the earth's capacity to support its growing population, we must therefore take into account other things besides statistics. Buddha, Confucius, Plato, Aristotle, Jesus, St. Paul, St. Augustine, and Pascal were all, according to the modern Western scale of values, members of underdeveloped nations.

When we are measuring the earth's capacity to feed its entire population, it is not enough to examine the deficiencies and potentialities in world terms. We must examine humanity people by people and country by country, continent by continent, and, while accepting the fact that progress will inevitably be slow, endeavor to describe the methods which will ensure this progress with continuity. We must also recognize that the particular effort to be undertaken in each separate country will have to take account of all the relevant factors.

Different is the case of Egypt, a country which has certainly been pressed to the limit of its resources on the narrow strip of cultivated land which borders the Nile. Different is the case of Algeria, which can live only "in tandem" with a European country which is capable of providing employment for its surplus workers. Different is the case of Haiti, which has hardly any arable soil, and also that of Black Africa, where a jigsaw puzzle system of different races inhabits land which is brittle and friable. Different is the case of the four former Indo-Chinese countries which possess, together, enough complementary resources to form an economic unit, but who are now obliged to depend heavily on aid from abroad. There is also the case of Chile, whose narrow Mediterranean plain is sandwiched between a complete desert and mountain glaciers, and whose mineral wealth is exploited by foreigners. There is the case of Iraq which could, through irrigation and by virtue of its oil royalties, reclaim the desert. There is the case of Saudi Arabia, which also has considerable oil royalties, but which is one of the most difficult countries to put to good use. There is the case of Colombia, which still possesses so many untapped resources. And there is the case of Brazil, a dominion as big as a continent, whose Amazon forest remains impenetrable.

It is therefore true that in each of these cases a uniform, standardized type of aid would be at a loss as to how to deal with the individual situation for which no simplified economic model holds good.

It is not a question of standardizing the world, but of taking each area with its human population and transforming potentialities into possibilities, and then into realities, in the rhythm of what is possible and with an uninterrupted series of small but significant advances. There will still be, however, some desperate cases whose plight can be alleviated and solved only through the disinterested generosity of the wealthier nations.

Finally, it appears useless to try to estimate humanity's chances of providing for the needs of a world population 2 or 3 times its present size. In the light of the problems caused by the settlement of migratory families and the transport of food supplies, there is still no universal solution. The world has to be analyzed as a series of restricted units, and as a series of regions which have to be formed into economically viable and balanced production units. The world must be analyzed with precision so that shortages and surpluses can be detected, and so that ways of improvement can be found which are at the same time easy and practical, taking all relevant circumstances into account.[3]

What is certain is that progress is both necessary and possible everywhere. But this progress demands strict co-operation between rich countries and poor countries. It is equally certain that the former have the duty to inaugurate or continue an effort which is to be increasingly aware of the possibilities and obstacles present, and that the latter have an enormous potential for helping in this field which can be used with more political and economic skill than in the past.

[3] A penetrating discussion of the problems and potential achievements of world-wide development may be found in the study of Michel Cépède, François Houtart and Linus Grond, *Population and Food* (New York: Sheed and Ward, 1964), pp. 357–461.

17

Cooperation Is Necessary

*The West can survive only if it becomes
a West without barriers.*

The traditional relationship between colonizer and colonized
is well known. The colony has to assume the role of both
reservoir and outlet. In its role as an outlet for the industrial
products of the parent country, it has to abjure all industrial
development itself. Insofar as it is a reservoir for commodities needed by the parent country, it is often exploited
in an irrational manner. Exploited—for that is the word—
by a form of capitalism whose aim is simply rapid profit, and
by countries which create a monopoly of the trade in or
production of certain raw materials (primarily agricultural
ones) on which the extremely vulnerable economy of these
nations depends to an ever-increasing extent.

The fact is that the more powerful societies evaluate the
fact of underdevelopment only in its relation to themselves.
They see it first of all as presenting an opportunity for their
own expansion; they see the possibility of laying their hands
on the unexploited or at least underexploited wealth in the
underdeveloped countries which is indispensable to their
industries; and they see the possibility of creating a market

for their own manufactured goods. They justify their pressure, which is at first economic and later political, by pointing to the immobility of both society and culture in these insufficiently developed countries.

This attitude has been responsible for everything that occurred during the old colonial era, and for everything which continues to happen under the wing of the more sophisticated forms of colonialism which are practiced by the dominant countries today, and particularly by the United States.

But what about President Truman's Point IV? Did not the American President on January 20, 1949 awaken American consciences to the task of helping people "to produce, through their own efforts, more food, more material to help build their houses, and more energy to lighten their burden"?

He was dealing, it appears, with a massive and unselfish plan which, if it had been adopted, would have changed the course of history. But it was inconsistent with the general mentality of the time, which was still completely impregnated with the facile dogma of a limited, self-centered form of capitalism.

Americans continue to express surprise when they discover that their interventions on behalf of the underdeveloped nations (which they consider to be benevolent and which indeed are partially so) breed a slight but noticeable amount of resentment everywhere. This is because they have created a new form of colonialism, as odious as the original colonialism and even less imbued with respect and love. The people whom they help are not slow to realize that they are of interest not for their own sakes, but as a function of the American network of strategic bases, or because they can fill a gap in the anti-Communist front, or because they

can provide the raw material and energy-producing substances needed by United States industry to ensure substantial dividends.

These people feel, therefore, that they are being exploited,
and that they are despised just as much as they were by the
original colonialists. Very often, they count less as a nation,
than as a means to American security and prosperity.

The United States seems to be making only a gracious
gesture to the countries of Europe when it declares that it
does not want to occupy an exclusive place in Africa.

Can it be denied that force of circumstances compels the
U.S.A. to exercise "leadership" of the anti-Communist countries? The unhappy aspect of it all—and it is a cause for
unease—is that the U.S.A. frequently acts without taking into
account either the real needs of the rest of humanity or the
urgent necessity for revising its own fundamental economic
and political concepts.

The future of the world, as we know, depends on American
decisions. We would prefer these decisions to be genuinely
intelligent and generous. And intelligence consists of understanding that today generosity alone is realistic.

Economic analysis shows that cooperation between the
advanced and the underdeveloped countries is possible. It is
both possible and necessary, because this alone can meet the
requirements of this century's basic problem.

According to experts of the United Nations, the effort
made on behalf of the underdeveloped countries by the more
advanced countries could, without reducing the standard of
living in the latter countries, or reducing it only by very
little, reach or exceed a figure of 13 billion dollars a year in
grants, loans and investment.

Western Europe, the United States, Canada, and Australia

could, if they were united with a view to improving the world situation, raise between 7 and 8 billion dollars by a special levy of as little as 2 per cent from their total income, which amounts to more than 350 billion. There is nothing extravagant in such a hypothesis. The United Kingdom exported 7 per cent of its national income between 1905 and 1913. The United States, without compromising its increasing prosperity, appropriated 3 per cent of its national income to gifts and loans. But we must do better than this. The political objectives themselves will have to be revised. "Armament," as an objective, must give way to "development." Is not one of the paradoxes of the present situation the discrepancy between the resources available for global development and those spent on preparation for an eventual world war?

If we consider this in the light of the national balance sheets for different countries, military expenditure in 1957–1958 represented:

	% of Gross National Product
United States	10.2
Great Britain	7.3
France	8.1
U.S.S.R.	15.5

The amount of money directly expended on military projects in the U.S.S.R. during recent years can be estimated at 96 billion rubles, which corresponds to the annual salaries of some 12 million workers. It is almost as high as the figure for the United States.

From these figures alone we can judge the enormous resources which are at the disposal of a world at peace for the betterment of the condition of its population.

It does not seem an exaggeration to estimate the total expenditure on what is known as "defense" throughout the world as something in the region of $100 billion. It should be noted that France alone spends almost $3 billion. England, for its part, spends $4.5 billion. We must also take into account money spent on military preparations in the countries attached to the alliances in both Western and Eastern hemispheres, as well as in the neutral countries.

This picture of a world which dissipates on preparations for destruction funds that could be used to avert hunger inspires François Perroux with a "great hope":

The effort for rearmament reveals the magnitude of the sacrifice of which the West becomes capable when it believes that the object of its sacrifice is vital. Rearmament in fact involves very many of the same gestures and actions that would be involved in the development of a trade economy.

The amount of effort needed to provide for the continuance of life is very much less than the amount which is being effectively prepared for massacre. The technical questions which have to be solved to ensure the survival of the species, are the same questions which have to be empirically resolved in order to organize the preparations for war. Machinery has already been prepared which, instead of destroying, can protect men and increase harvests.[*]

[*] *L'Europe sans rivages, op. cit.,* p. 408. Cf. also the remarks of Pope Paul VI on the conditions necessary for world peace, in his Christmas Message of 1963.

But this great hope can be entertained only if men's consciences develop at the same time. Certain reactions can only fill one with disquiet. There is that of Pierre Gaxotte in *Le Figaro* on October 1, 1956, as an example of this:

We are told that we must help the underdeveloped countries, and send them money for investment, books and men. We have been doing nothing but this for the last hundred years. By continuing to do it we will only lose our money and make enemies of those who are under an obligation to us. This is quite natural. Nothing is more onerous than gratitude. A developing people comes to hate its instructors because their presence is humiliating. Leave the backward countries alone. Let them evolve in their own way and by themselves, without upsetting their way of thinking and feeling as a result of bringing them a civilization which is foreign to them, a technical skill which they themselves have not created, and a science which they have not discovered. Is what I am saying terrible? It is quite possible. But history is full of terrible things. When I was at primary school, I was made to put aside one *sou* every week to save the little Chinese children whose parents, we were told, otherwise gave them to the pigs for want of other food. Have I saved Chinese children? I hope not, because these Chinese children, when they grew up, came to Dien Bien Phu and killed thousands of Frenchmen.

Gaxotte's philosophy is certainly somewhat limited, even when he claims to speak from motives of self-interest. He has certainly not considered the figures which demonstrate the developed countries' dependence on the underdeveloped countries for raw materials and fuel and as outlets for manufactured products.

The question of opportunities for development is no longer asked, because the earth has become too small to allow the partitions that exist to remain hermetically sealed. World opinion will not allow millions of men to remain at the mercy of a deadly epidemic or famine without making some kind of a gesture of help. The question is not one of whether it is a good idea to encourage or impede development, but of finding out in what conditions development is possible, and in attempting to find the best possible form of development. There are irreversible movements in history. In the last century, for instance, Marx analyzed the relationship between management and workers, and this analysis proved decisive in the development of trade-unionism and social progress. The work of international experts has had a similar influence. These tend to modify the form of the relationship between the developed and the underdeveloped countries.

The desire for universal justice, however confused it may appear to be, is a comparatively recent phenomenon in mankind taken as a whole; and, if the nations imbued with the Christian ideal have carried the germ of it, their influential people have never formulated it with as much vigor as they do today. In spite of all the deviations from the ideal and in spite of attempts to counterfeit it, the right of all men to participate in the fruits of the earth in order to meet their essential needs, is nowadays accepted both formally and tacitly.

The slowness of the West in drawing the necessary conclusions from this is explained less by any basic ill will than by the lack of objective information and by the influence of economic institutions which are based exclusively on the profit motive, as well as by that of political institutions colored by unrelieved nationalism and imbued with imperialistic traditions.

However serious this tardiness may be, it is not an obstinate refusal. No matter what the West does, its privileged position is going to become less and less comfortable. Its dependence on the rest of the world can only be intensified. Its elementary ideology of justice can only be improved and extended; but this, as it happens, will reinforce the needs of the countries which remain hungry. When the West finds itself obliged, as it will, to intervene in the domestic affairs of countries which are threatened with social and economic disintegration, or to defend countries which are threatened by avaricious neighbors, it will be forced to develop a clearer conscience about collective world responsibilities.

Even the American Congress will not be able to preserve its narrow, pragmatic mentality indefinitely. As it remains one of the two major powers in the world and discovers the rapidity with which it can provoke resentment, the United States cannot lag behind in evaluating the true nature of the problem.

It is therefore clear that if the West resists the change which is being imposed on it, this rejection will be suicidal. Internal dissension has destroyed the capacity of the European countries for conquering other nations and occupying them permanently; and the Americans have experienced in Korea, as have the French in Vietnam and in Algeria, their incapacity for subduing a people who are determined to affirm their nationalities at all costs, even if it means calling on help from abroad.

The West can protect itself only by abandoning its introspective attitude. If it is not capable of providing the remaining underdeveloped countries which are independent of Russia, in a clear-cut fashion and with disinterested idealism, with more and better chances of integrated development than are afforded to the underdeveloped areas of the satellite republics of the U.S.S.R., it can be sure that its pragmatic, materialistic philosophy will enlist a much smaller following than Marxism which, although it is philosophically material- istic, is imbued with a universal ideal.

If the West lags behind in developing its conscientious awareness of the total needs of mankind and slows down its already quickening response to these needs, it will condemn itself to slavery. In the final analysis, the only way for the West to save itself is through self-improvement and by dis- engaging every kind of greed from the spheres of action it occupies in order to attain the sincerity of altruism.

The hatred felt for the West, and for the United States in particular, is less than the hatred of the hungry for the rich— although this, of course, does enter into it to some extent —but the hatred of those who are scorned, disrespected, and unloved for those who should have loved them. If it does not develop within itself a universal, brotherly love, the West will be irretrievably condemned.

A complete revolution, perhaps man's last and greatest one, has become necessary. It will be more long-drawn-out than others of the past, because it must be universal. It is both a political and an economic revolution; but it can come to its fulfilment only if it is primarily a spiritual revolution—the expression of consideration for others because of their actual or potential value as human beings.

Will the West be able to effect its conversion to this uni- versal spirituality in time?

The Soviet world, in spite of its campaigns for peace, is at least as responsible as the United States for the frantic armaments race and the consequent inability on the part of the rich countries to assist the poorer ones. Its advantage is that the Marxist doctrine which it vaunts is deliberately a world-wide one; it envisages the total liberation of all the proletariat, liberation from capitalist exploitation, from man's domination by nature, and for the colonial countries, liberation from the colonialists.

Children who know no better, continue their argument, although an earthquake may be on the point of annihilating them. People are now playing while atomic war or the revolution of the rest of the world threatens them with total extinction, invasion or occupation.

Part Six

Demands Made by a New Civilization:
A NEW CIVILIZATION AND
THE DYNAMIC FORCES IN EXISTENCE

*None of the great dynamic forces in
existence today is immediately ready to
fulfil the requirements of a new
civilization.*

The problem facing the world today is that of creating a
new civilization. Is a divided mankind ready to evaluate its
condition in the most realistic manner possible? Is it, apart
from technical uniformity, prepared to respect legitimate differences and man's right to full liberty? Can it define and promote the collective good of mankind?

Human intelligence has already shown us what it is capable of in the spheres of mathematics, physics, biology, and
technology. Is it now capable of building up a system of
thought and methods of assistance that will control and
direct global development by integrating the human and
social sciences? Are the tremendous forces which are now
massing to attack the world enough to ensure that this very
difficult effort will be made, and that this very rewarding success will be won? This is what we have to examine now.

18

American Immaturity

"We asked you for hope, understanding and love, and you gave us money and technology. Are these the things which account for your country's greatness?"

Bert F. Hoselitz, the American sociologist, has explained the reason why the United States has not shown, up to the present, the maturity needed to accomplish this task, a task which it should be the first to undertake. The puritanism which presided over the birth of the United States has been toned down little by little. In the public eye material success has taken the place of work as the fundamental value. Money has become the yardstick of everything.

This has produced a situation where determining values are ascribed to the material and tangible aspects of civilization. Otherwise how can we explain the fact that many Americans are more concerned with the size and architectural solidity of their schools than with what is taught within their walls? How otherwise can we understand the numerous dangers to which television, as well as illustrated criminal adventure stories, expose children every day, all for profit? If there is a conflict between the norms of art, education or culture on the one hand, and the demands of material profit on the other, the latter almost invariably have an easy victory.

In the present political situation in which the United States is at the head of the anti-Communist bloc, one feels the need for a doctrine which can better Communist ideology on the international level. Some people think that this doctrine is embodied in American capitalism, because of the success which has attended its efforts in the sphere of material production. But this success is due only to some very special historical factors, and we must not be surprised to discover that other countries do not share in American ideology purely and simply, and in fact show hardly any inclination to adopt it. The American theory of capitalism, precisely because it considers the material success of the individual as the highest pinnacle of achievement, can have no attraction for the masses of people in Asia and Africa for whom the material success of the white man and colonialist exploitation have often gone hand in hand.

The United States is on the horns of a particularly serious dilemma. In the first place, it must accept its responsibilities as a leader. In the second place, however, every formula for progress which seemed to have such beneficial results in the United States is now revealed to be inapplicable elsewhere. Even the dynamism of the U.S. economy will not allow it to retreat into an isolationist position. The United States needs the rest of the world as a market for its products as well as a source of raw materials and fuel substances without which its economic machinery can no longer function. Its spirit, though, does not seem to match up to the responsibilities that appear in the wake of material domination.

The following plea addressed to one American expert enables us to evaluate this discrepancy between ideal and practice. It was made in 1953 by an official of one of the Southeast Asian countries which were benefiting under Point IV. "We asked you," he said, "for hope, understanding and love, and you gave us money and technology. Are these the things which account for your country's greatness?" It is a pity that American understanding of and love for other people is expressed in such de-spiritualized terms. The United States often seems to lack the kind of culture that is in effect the harmonious acquisition of various forms of knowledge which permits the understanding of humanity. In spite of its undeniable good will, the United States has not yet acquired the width and depth of vision which would encourage us to adhere unconditionally to its leadership. It is prepared, in perfect good faith, to launch the world into the most terrible adventures imaginable, while its magnificent but often disconnected and dehumanized contributions to economics and sociology fail to help it to understand that if it continues to make the mistakes it is making at present, the United States is contributing more to the disintegration of the world than to a universal unity based on farsighted and brotherly cooperation.

The task before the United States since 1945 has been to respect other nations while associating them in an amicable manner in the most wide-ranging plan for civilization, and not to stir up dishonestly a crusade for objectives devoid of any authentic spiritual value. The Americans are again beginning to make the mistake of the bourgeois who confused their own condition with that of their country, and who insisted that the essential criterion of the social order should be at least the maintenance of the status quo, if not the augmentation of their own privileges.

Americans have—and they are right to have—a sharpened consciousness of the dangers facing the world through the universal spread of Communism. But one can legitimately ask whether, in the final analysis, they are not the most efficient promoters of it owing to their own sheer inflexibility. The acuteness of East-West tension is the result, in part, of the narrowness of the American outlook. By focusing Western strength on "defense" to an excessive degree, instead of deliberately bringing about an effective and general defense against hunger—even if it involves sacrifices affecting its standard of living—the United States is provoking an intensified opposition to "defense" of the wrong sort.

19

Marxism: the Illusory Solution

*If Marx had continued to investigate man and
civilization with the same fervour as that with
which he investigated economics, Marxism
would not perhaps be the inhuman thing it
now is.*

—Emmanuel Mounier

The United States then is not yet mature enough to succeed
in the lengthy and difficult task of establishing a civilization
based on the common brotherhood of all men. Can Marxism,
perhaps, save each man and mankind as a whole? Here too
we must reply "No"; and this even further aggravates the
crisis of this century. Marxist humanism, in fact, is basically
vitiated by its metaphysical atheism. Even if Marxism has
permitted the development of a country as great as the
U.S.S.R., it is nevertheless unable to found a permanent and
authentically human civilization because it is basically un-
aware of the essence of mankind.

It is not difficult to understand that in this short book we
cannot devote ourselves to the deep analysis of Marxism
which alone would allow us to provide a fully accurate and
valid basis for our conclusions. The few remarks which fol-

low have nevertheless seemed to us to be necessary in order to make understood the attraction of Communism and the gravity of the threat which faces the Western world and the entire human race.

MARXISM AS A DEVELOPMENT TECHNIQUE

Marx's vision, although prophetic, led too quickly to the Communist system. Lenin, Marx's disciple, believed too early that the moment for revolution had arrived. In Marx's view, the revolution had to be a universal one. Universal capitalism had to give way to the universality of the proletariat.

The growing concentration of capital ensured not only the effectiveness of its domination, but the proximity and inevitability of its decline. So he reasoned. The proletariat had to seize political and economic power at the same time.

Things did not turn out in this way, however. Lenin believed that by starting the revolution in one country alone— a country which was not yet fully industrialized—the infection of revolution would spread to the industrialized nations. Nothing of the kind happened and emergent Communism found itself off balance in one country and wishing, nevertheless, to be successful at any price. This is the drama in which we are taking part now.

The type of Communism which was established in Russia was able, through the cleverness of its alliances, its diplomacy and its intrigues, to take over a large slice of Eastern Europe. Since then, with the completion of a campaign which it initiated years ago in Asia, it has been able to infect China,

North Korea, and Viet Nam. Today it is preparing to annex other portions of South and Southeast Asia.

The Communist regime's first phase was a naïve one. In *The State and Revolution* Lenin outlined his idea of the revolution in oversimplified terms. The assumption of power and the immediate control of the economy by the workers, with a simultaneous reduction of all wages to the level of that of the worker, seemed essentially a simple operation to carry out successfully. In fact, the economic regression was emphasized, and the leaders of the revolution were therefore placed in a desperate situation. They had to go backwards, and a "new political economy" had to be elaborated. Luckily for them a breathing space was gained. The first experiment was halted while there was still time to profit from the original economic structure by maintaining in part private property in the sphere of means of production and of free trading. But this was only a stage. When Stalin arrived, the transition to the decisive stage took place by the introduction of planning.

Planning, which was unanimously declared by orthodox economists to be unworkable, brought into existence an economy without a real market. By merely existing, the collectivist regime proved that it could exist. This was of tremendous significance. Private property in the means of production was reduced to almost nothing; there was a small artisan population, and each peasant had a small piece of land surrounding the family house.

This creation, however, was not brought into being without impediments or setbacks. The evidence for some of these has been given in newspapers, magazines, and elsewhere. The system needed criticism in order to help it correct itself.

In such a huge system of planning, some forms of waste would not be immediately apparent to those responsible. Criticism, when it is expressed in the press, ensures the speediest intervention to readjust the working of the machine or the economic structure itself.

Russia therefore was in a privileged position where development was concerned. It had an immense country at its disposal, and one with an enormous potential. Power can choose the level on which it will function most effectively. The State, judge of the total work requirement that will have to be levied, is also the judge of the distribution of its assessments between different sectors of investment: the sub-structures, basic industry, manufacturing and service industries. The assessment level of the "plus-value" is considerably more important in Russia than in any capitalist country whatsoever. The State is the sole arbiter of the ratio between consumption and investment. It can always adapt its judgment to the general premises of its policy, whether it is one of development or "defense." The State is the only master, whether its actions involve the inauguration of a policy designed to create powerful production facilities as a means to total development, or whether they involve the production of massive quantities of armaments in the face of danger from an adversary. It is also the sole arbiter when it comes to choosing the most favorable regions for industrial development. It can choose the areas in its vast territory where all the elements for powerful industrialization are combined: hydroelectric power, coal, steel, and manganese. In this way it can bring to fruition its huge combined operations which surpass the greatest free enterprises in the West. Furthermore—and this is of considerable importance—Russia ad-

heres to a rigid system of police restraint to ensure the continuance of the regime. A nation which has always been
accustomed to an attitude of resigned passivity, and one
which has never authentically experienced true freedom,
yields easily to this concept of political and economic life.

Circumstances have permitted an economic success based
on rapid exploitation in spite of setbacks, the most important
of which is the inadequate production of livestock. One
diplomat just returned from Moscow in 1951 told us: "In
twenty years the Russians will perhaps invite the West to
recognize the secret of their success by seeing it for themselves." Today the invitations come thick and fast, without
however allowing visitors any opportunity to note the de-
fects in the system. One must look at things dispassionately.
In strictly economic terms the massive setback which had
been expected has not occurred. On the contrary, despite
tentative efforts and occasional reversals, and not without
threats of future failure, first Eastern Europe and then a large
part of Asia have experienced a considerable amount of development. The development techniques which were first
used in Russia itself, were later continued in several economically underdeveloped or undeveloped countries, these
being perfected and adapted in the process. The West will
gain nothing by closing its eyes to all this, and even less now
that the eyes of the people in the underdeveloped countries
are turned more frequently towards the East. Communism
has systematically undertaken the conquest of the world, and
avails itself of every favorable opportunity to consolidate its
advance wherever it can.

Can we conclude from this that the Soviet experiment is
going to sweep the world immediately? The U.S.S.R. has al-

ready brought more than 1 billion people within its sphere
of influence, 700 million of these being Chinese. If Russian
industry is to provide the necessary equipment for the development of this super-empire, it will, economically speaking,
have to speed up its rate of growth even more. Technicians
in sufficient numbers for these huge countries are simply not
available at the moment. They will have to wait for them.
Russia does not feel at the moment that it is in a position to
take over the world completely. It has to proceed stage by
stage, while at the same time taking care not to provoke any
war in which it would be directly engaged. As time is on
Russia's side, the moment will come when additional annexa-
tions can be made. Peace works for the communization of
the world inasmuch as the West—and particularly Western
capitalism—fails to understand the significance of the discontent of the underdeveloped countries, and the ease with
which Communists disseminate their propaganda in them.
Through capitalism's ignorance of the methods necessary to
save the world by modifying it in depth, everything combines to leave the world in the state of mind in which it longs
for the relief which Communism might bring. Russian strategy is to leave all to time; to build up their super-empire and
the network of countries which they are preparing to take
over: Japan slowly, but South Vietnam and Burma more
quickly, and also Ceylon and Indonesia. The difficulty for
Russia will be that of swallowing India when the time comes.
A population growth of up to 1 billion in the East calls for
a stage of economic growth which has not yet been reached.
Around 1952, one of the senior officials in the Russian
economic administration was asked: "If the West left all
the underdeveloped countries of the world in your hands,

would you be capable of developing the world properly?"
His answer was: "No, no." Russian strategy is aware that
there have to be interim stages.

The Islamic nations to the south of Russia can present a
certain amount of resistance to communization, and England
has attempted to strengthen this tendency by the Baghdad
Pact, which is both a military and an economic agreement.
The Suez affair, however, greatly affected this, and now the
United States is attempting to take Britain's place by doling
out lavish grants. Russia's answer to the Colombo Pact and
American aid is to help the underdeveloped countries also.
The internal dissension in Iran, the growth of Communism
in Iraq in spite of governmental prohibitions, and the strength
of Communism in Egypt in spite of Nasser's originally re-
actionary attitude, all lead little by little to growing acceptance of the idea of Russian aid. This creates favorable opportunities for Soviet expansion, while at the same time the
countries of Europe are not immune. Italy has appeared, at
one stage, ripe for the plucking, and France is being worked
on continuously. All this has prepared the way for the acquisition of a large part of Southeast Asia. We are not concerned here with the Scandinavian countries, which would
be incapable of defending themselves in a case of aggression.
They have already passed through the socialist stage which
has been reached by Communism through suppressing class
tension almost completely. Further afield bridgeheads are
being formed, particularly in Africa, around the mining dis-
tricts of the center and the southeast, and also in the most
industralized countries of Latin America: Brazil, Chile, Colombia, and Mexico. Troops, as it were, are being deployed
on wider fronts everywhere, even in the countries which

seem to be most antipathetic to Communism. The Americans talked much some ten years ago of Communist infiltration even in their diplomatic service. Everyone is aware that there is an active Communist force in Canada. Russia is waiting for her efforts to bear fruit; her grand campaign for peace is easily explained. For peace, even if it is broken by occasional incidents—perhaps by partial wars involving China, for example—favors a world-wide Soviet victory.

MARXISM AS HUMANISM

Marxism, insofar as it consists of an ideology of economic development, encourages a healthy and necessary trend. But this ideology includes a spurious humanism which provides no sure guidance for the solution of present-day human problems. As Maritain said, with justification, in his *Humanisme intégral:* "Marx saw that the class struggle was the effective consequence of the capitalist system, and that the great historical task of modern times was the emancipation of the proletariat. But he marred this insight with his theory of inevitable and irreconcilable class warfare, and with a false philosophy of both man and work which amounted to the socialization of the entire human being."

Marx, who was a disciple of Hegel, wanted to set Hegel "back on his feet." Hegel's complex philosophy presented a sort of dialectical immanence in which the divine element progressively impregnated all earthly forms of reality until it became incarnate in the State, and particularly in the Prussian state. Marxism established itself as a philosophical doctrine in reaction against the position adopted by a false spirituality. Marx, however, retained dialectical analysis as a means of acquiring knowledge: thesis, antithesis and synthesis. He replaced the synthesis by the "leap"—a catastrophe giving rise to a new situation in which the antithesis has won control. In history Marx's philosophy is, essentially, a dynamic of evolution through tension.

Marx affirmed his own rigorous materialism in preference to the idealism of his master. In this materialism his principle was that there was no idea before matter, before nature. The idea appeared with the growth, during evolution, of man's capacity for thought. Man, who is subject, became aware of objects, and knowledge consisted of this fusion between subject and object.

"Today," said Marx, "there cannot possibly be room in our evolutionary concept of the world for a Creator and an Orderer." Man, to be precise, was no more than a transitory element of nature. The advance of mankind and its triumph over the world was all that mattered. Each man was, in the midst of the great mass of humanity, equal only to one point, one moment. He could not achieve immortality.

"Apart from nature and mankind," wrote Engels, "there is nothing, and the superior beings created by our religious imaginations are only the fantastic reflections of our own selves."

In this way, religion was no more than a "conception of man's alienated self," and the most serious of the three fundamental feelings of alienation which formed a chain: the sense of alienation felt by the worker, frustrated by the sight of all his productive work benefiting the capitalist and the bourgeois; the sense of alienation also felt by the worker and induced in him by the absence of his liberty, by which he is made the slave of capitalism; and the sense of alienation felt by the man who feels that he is enslaved to a divine chimera.

It was also implied that men are only the products of the natural order, which is itself transformed by men; and religion by its very essence empties man and nature of all their content, and transfers this content to a phantom god in a world beyond, who graciously returns a part of his superfluity to man and to nature.

Marxist materialism is a radical materialism. The spirit is not denied; but the activities which we ascribe to the human spirit can only be the properties of living matter which has reached a certain point in complexity.

In his criticism of Hegel, Marx lacked the concepts of analogy and transcendence; and the author of *Das Kapital* considers that all that exists is matter. His humanism, consequently, is a mutilated form of humanism. Even though he may use the word "man" here and there, man has in fact faded out of the picture.

With Lenin we arrive at the practical phase of the revolution. The revolutionary struggle, through its strategic and tactical perspective and controlled by the Party, should crush all opposition.

Revolution is the most authoritative thing possible. . . . The existence of factions is incompatible with party unity. . . . The party must have iron discipline.

The dictatorship of the proletariat, which is a necessary sequel to the Revolution in order to purify the new regime of all the bourgeois after-effects of the previous one, is a desperate fight, bloody and yet bloodless, violent and yet pacific, military and economic, academic and administrative, against the traditions and power of the old forms of society.

Pity has no place here, nor truth in the normal sense of the word. Truth is what makes the revolution progress and succeed. We are thus plunged into a state of anti-humanism. All opposition is criminal, and anyone who opposes the regime must be prevented, by killing him if necessary, from halting the forward march of mankind whose only authorized representative is the Party. Religion, the conservative influence of the past, must be relegated to its place along with the other, useless things; more than that, it must be beaten down by vigorous propaganda.

Man, thus freed, is more than ever bound to the sub-human. A new religion—that of the progress of humanity—will replace the old. Established materialism leads logically to the sole triumph of the proletariat. A religion of unlimited progress, of one class bearing all the hopes of the world on its shoulders, and the creed of universal liberation, make mankind man's real god, his only acceptable god.

Barbarism therefore is at our gates, however technically competent it may be, however capable it shows itself to be of developing the resources of the earth above and below ground. Man, snatched up to form part of the huge production machine, can no longer be man. After what seems to be a period of great progress, he finds himself facing a void.

This anti-humanism cannot prolong itself indefinitely. Sooner or later the human conscience will have its revival. If the West, cleansed of its wicked passions, were to give a pure witness to the Gospel through an intelligent and vigorous campaign, by assuming responsibility for the control of the "deprived" world, the shock would be so great that, in the East, it would change the whole world trend. But as long as the West continues to oppose the humanitarian spirit of Communism with nothing but greedy calculations and a lack of social consciousness despite its atomic superiority, so long will the Marxist god progressively invade the world.

What is striking about Marxism, when it has been reduced to its essential traits, is the fact that it seems to be completely coherent, undivided by schism, and the fact that it claims to have a solution for every problem and is both dynamic and capable of world-wide application.

To anyone who is dissatisfied with capitalist society, it offers the opportunity of revolt; to the deprived it holds out hope of better days; to the oppressed it offers capacity for resistance; to the isolated it offers the strength of the proletariat, the savior of humanity. To the man who is devoid of culture it offers a philosophy of history and an economic and sociological system; to the potential leader it offers the leitmotif of the crystallization of one group; to the ambitious it offers the possibility of success through the support of the masses who are waiting to be organized.

A man moved by a sense of elementary justice which he feels to be lacking in the world can be inspired by Communism; the hesitant intellectual will discover his doctrine in it; the non-believer will discover the new religion of humanity acquiring divinity through his own efforts; and the lukewarm believer will find it easy to transfer his affection to it.

These latter cases still occur even in the West, which still has something left of the Christian spirit. According as they continue to give way before the Western form of logic which has been adopted since the technological and scientific revolution, superstitious practices, myths, sorcery, or magic arts which have become too ridiculous or too oppressive, and other naïve beliefs, will readily yield place to the great myth of a liberated humanity without any trace of social sin.

Communism, offering a mystique of materialism to mankind materialized but lacking a philosophy, finds possibilities of penetration on every side. It inspires revolutionary enthusiasm in peoples who were previously resigned and passive. The ignorant peasant is content to grasp, without fully understanding them, the broad outlines of the struggle against poverty and oppression. As soon as he progresses, he is captivated by what he hears of the achievements of the U.S.S.R. Later, he perceives the possibility of equating his nationalistic pride with his frustration at not yet having attained the place in the world to which he believes himself entitled. With education, he has discovered a philosophy of the universe.

In this way, all religious alienation is forced to give place to the cult of mankind becoming ruler of the earth.

Until now the West has not taken sufficient precautions against the disadvantages of its position. While its selfishness and its mistakes are exposed to the full light of day, the flaws in the Soviet structure remain masked. Communist propaganda, whether it is permitted, hindered or actually forbidden, operates in the heart of the West, while the West is unable to penetrate the officially Marxist part of the world. While Western techniques for developing the underdeveloped countries are negated or dominated by the interests of individuals or groups and show themselves to be powerless, the apparatus and resources of the Russian solution (an almost integral system of planning) or the continued mobilization of the basic group of volunteers animated and coordinated by one driving force (the Party bound up with the

State) which is the Chinese solution, permit rapid and coherent economic progress. The Chinese "vital activists," continually fixing the solid targets of the common good, are
trained to deal with difficult situations by raising a collective
and mobile force to deal with them. It can consist equally
well of a campaign against flies, mosquitoes or birds, or of
one against the plague, smallpox or famine. These simple objectives which are readily apparent to all, easily command
respect, much more so than if they formed part of a grandiose
scheme. Such a scheme, however, is not lacking where the
most general problems and those detected by serious analysis
are concerned.

MARXISM AND A NEW CIVILIZATION

When we consider the facts, both the United States and
Russia, the two nations fated to compete for world domination, appear as colossi with feet of clay. By underestimating
mankind they have sapped the foundations of any durable
success they might have achieved. The forms of civilization
that they advocate will not create a world-wide civilization.

While the United States weakens itself and others by destroying the last remaining vestiges of European trust and
by breaking down in a few years the confidence that people
were so willing to give, the U.S.S.R. is witnessing an increase
in the number of contradictions both in its own internal
system and in its imperialistic structure.

Moscow fears China with an obsessive fear. The social
classes are being re-formed; groups of young, privileged and
idle people are appearing; the students give Marxist teaching a cool welcome; the great mass of the population is dis-

satisfied with the ratio between consumption and investment and would like it to favor the former more. The peasants, terrified of the army of which they form the essential part including officers, recoil at the transformation of the kolkhozes into larger collective units which are even more dependent on power.

Religious feeling seems to be undergoing a re-birth. Yugoslavia has separated itself to some extent from Russia; Hungary has rebelled; and Poland has won, for a time, a more respected and independent position. Outside this empire, the Communist parties are growing tired of contradictory exhortations, and are beginning to suspect that they are on the wrong path.

The warlike confrontation of the two power blocs would not achieve anything, no matter who won, even supposing that the intensive use of atomic weapons does not put the entire Northern hemisphere in mortal danger. After such a war is over, the causes of world malaise would be only more virulent; the less favored sections of the wealthy nations would have been impoverished even further, and aid to the poorer countries would have ceased completely. Even if we were to assume that the Communist governments would be overthrown, their ideology of class revolt and national revolt would probably be only temporarily contained by such a victory. The world, which would perhaps be a great deal more anarchical, would have to be completely reorganized, and we can easily see what insurmountable difficulties would face those undertaking the task.

But in the meantime why do the two great powers still insist on fighting from indefensible positions? The Test Ban treaty signed on August 5, 1963, by the U.S.S.R., the

United States, and the United Kingdom, shows that when the interest of all is at stake, a policy of agreement between the opposing great powers is not *a priori* impossible. The West, admittedly, cannot afford to be naïve in the face of proposals from whatever part of the opposing front line. Communism is historically rooted in duplicity. Must one therefore conclude that it will always be so? Communism has already abandoned many of the ideas of Marx and Lenin, some of them important ones, when the evidence forced it to do so. Does it still think of boasting of Marx's position with regard to the family or Lenin's statements about the reward for work? Does it still think that the suppression of private property in the means of production is enough to make the State out of date, to annihilate religious feeling or to suppress moral deviations? Does it still believe that liberty springs from man's domination of nature?

Stalin, when he had grown old, described the limits of Marxism in an astonishing speech. Human intelligence, even in Marxist experience and also because of it, can make an issue again, for example, of Marx's anti-religious attitude, which was both tactical and metaphysical. Religious feeling which has been repressed or diverted towards illusory values can reappear as a personal and a social value. The concept of a purely dialectic and pragmatic truth can rapidly appear unacceptable to minds which have been taught scientific and technical objectivity.

It is essentially the same for the Russians and the Chinese as for the Americans. None of them would be able to annihilate the human soul and its capacity for reshaping itself even after it has been bombarded for years with oversimplifications. If the West were actually to acquire greater knowl-

edge of the world situation and of the ethical aspect of aid
—on which it continues to pride itself—and if it were, in
consequence, to revise the infantile economic dogmas which
have blinded its vision, the shock to the Communists, and
to that part of the world which favors the Communist camp,
would be enormous. They would be forced to undertake a
radical reappraisal of certain weak points in their narrow
philosophy and the unhealthy condition of their hateful
totalitarian political systems.

The West, as well as the East, can set itself the task of
understanding the naïveté and cruelty of some of its principles. Is the "grant economy," which it pursues so timidly,
beginning to make its first impression on the persistent
illusion that justice is satisfied with the payment of the price
which the developed countries impose on the world market?

If the West abandoned this iniquitous practice, it would
make it far harder for Russia to subordinate the collectivist
world to the arbitrary rules of its own dominant economy.

Some clear readjustment of views both in the East and in
the West would ensure the success of any move to end the
prolonged hesitations on both sides and undertake the
foundation of an economy which would be at the service of
mankind.

20

The Uncommitted Nations

*If Communism is bad, colonialism is
infinitely worse.*

—Jawaharlal Nehru

A third force has emerged in world affairs as a result of the
Bandung conferences.[1] Its area of influence extends, without
interruption, from the north of Japan to Black Africa. It is
partly included in the Communist-dominated world, being

[1] In April 1955, a group of Afro-Asian countries met in Bandung,
Indonesia, to discuss mutual problems. Numbering about twenty-nine,
they included such countries as Japan, Mainland China, North Vietnam, South Vietnam, Laos, Indonesia, Pakistan, India, Iran, Iraq,
Turkey, Saudi Arabia, and Egypt. Many of these countries were
formerly colonial territories, and were now eager to establish themselves as independent nations. Among the problems they discussed
were the effects of colonialist rule, the pressures of the Cold War,
racial equality, nonaggression, and the right of each nation to be free
from outside interference. In addition to the participating nations,
almost all the major powers of the world were represented by unoffi-
cial delegations or observers. Nine years later, in October, 1964, the
second meeting of the so-called "non-aligned" or "uncommitted" nations took place in Cairo, Egypt. Many of those nations that attended
the previous conference were again present at this second meeting.

bordered partly by that sphere of influence, and partly by the European-dominated areas of Southern Africa. The Bandung meetings did not at first sight appear to be more than a gesture by a group of malcontent countries who were as yet incapable of settling on a definite objective; but in fact they also signified the affirmation of these countries in favor of independence, which could become the will to revolt and form the point of departure for a complete change of attitude.

If Western observers were surprised by this, forewarned experts were not. One of these, Tibor Mende, wrote in *La Révolte de l'Asie:*

The majority of Asiatics have had no trouble in convincing themselves that the presence of foreign rulers in their countries had something to do with their retarded condition. Even those who lacked the intellectual equipment needed to evaluate the actions of the foreigners admitted instinctively that the presence of Westerners in Asia was dictated by economic interests.[2]

This highly-compressed book of Mende's should be read and re-read by anyone who wants to understand fully the explosion of resentment that took place at Bandung and the warmth with which Chou En-Lai, the Chinese representative, was welcomed. Pandit Nehru's statement in January 1951, "If Communism is bad, colonialism is infinitely worse," cannot be forgotten.

Everything, however, points to the fact that the "Bandung force" will not find it easy to coalesce into an organic bloc. It is a long way from northern Japan to Rhodesia and Mozam-

[2] Paris, Presses Universitaires de France, 1951, pp. 9, 10.

bique, and there are too many different civilizations included in this huge geographical figure of a reversed "S." The reverberations which followed its foundation will continue, however, to exercise considerable influence on the deliberations of the United Nations General Assembly and on its peace-keeping operations. As a voting power the "Bandung force" has a majority, and it would have a crushing superiority if the discontented nations of Latin America came to its support. The Western world, and the United Nations, have already had more than one opportunity of learning that the era of Western world domination is over.

The Suez affair was more than a symbol of this. We can remember the immense upheavals it produced in the Western economy and the huge waste of resources that it involved. Eleven million dollars to clear one canal. . . .

However, the underdeveloped segment of the world, which stretches to the south of the more industrialized countries, has such national and ethnic diversity that any agreement other than one for a negative purpose would seem impossible for the time being. Different ideologies and systems of thought jostle and clash with each other. The native religions vary between Shintoism and Animism, with intermediary stages of Taoism, Confucianism, Buddhism, Hinduism, Zoroastrianism, and Mohammedism. And each of these religions is subdivided into different branches, not to mention hundreds of sects. The search for one God, which could be the leaven in a united civilization, remains the preoccupation of the intellectual and spiritual élite. It has little or nothing to do with the huge masses of people who are enslaved to the widest imaginable range of superstitions.

Since Islam has failed to impose its own idea of God on

Buddhist or Hindu countries, it is illusory to imagine that the great religious cults of Asia will ever evolve together in harmony. This is already obvious from the weakness of Chinese Buddhism when faced with the Communist mystique, which is being propagated ceaselessly from one village to another throughout the country. The rapid extension of sheer materialism also has to be taken into account.

The half of the world which is made wretched by hunger will never be united for long by religion. It cannot by itself, or in any of its divisions, dominate the West, seeing that the West will, in spite of its internal dissensions, continue to unite to defend its privileges and what it considers to be its values. The hungry world can, however, one day, by sheer weight of numbers, and aided by China and Russia, burst in a wave all over Europe in the last, desperate gesture of starving men.

Still we should not ignore the contribution they could make to a new civilization. This would not be a civilization of wealth or of violence, nor one based on the fear of death. The sophisticated Western world must come to understand that the people on the other side of the fence are not savages, but only people with a different scale of values. The West can even learn from them the virtue of moderating one's desires.

Gandhi's store of wisdom is not only an Indian treasure. Every civilization can borrow from it and, what is more, find in it many of the most authentic Western values.

Sincerity must go hand in hand with wisdom. No one will then discriminate between any one community and another, between high-caste and low-caste. Every man will regard everyone else as his equal and will gather all to him in the silken net of his love. No one will consider anyone else to be "untouchable." The hard-working laborer and the capitalist will be considered as equals.

A life of sacrifice is the summit of art, and it is a life which is full of true joy. He who wishes to serve will not waste thoughts on his own personal comfort. This he will leave to his Master in heaven, who may or may not provide for him. He will not encumber himself, therefore, with everything that he finds on his way; he will take only what is strictly necessary and leave the rest. He will be calm, freed from anger, and his spirit will be at peace even if he is in trouble. His service, like his virtue, is his reward, and in it he will find his contentment.

Serving others voluntarily demands that everyone must give of his best and must be completely unselfish. In fact, the man who is genuinely religious consecrates himself unreservedly to the service of humanity.[3]

One could find hundreds of quotations like these which could be reflected upon with advantage by political and economic leaders both in the West and in the East. Many lessons could also be learned from them by the leaders of the newly independent countries, and by the technical assistants who are sent to these countries. This is the reason for the affirmation that "true democracy cannot be the work of twenty men united at one point; it must be the work undertaken from the very lowest level by the population of every village."

Gandhi's work is being continued by Vinoba, who is persuading the large landowners, whom he enlists from one village to another, to distribute their lands of their own

[3] M. K. Gandhi, *The Welfare of All* (Ahmedabad: Navajivan, 1954).

accord. For him the lives of the workers must be so happy that others will envy their lot, and students must be trained to pass on the benefits of their education to the whole people.

If the West, puffed up with its own importance, were to ignore this Asian experiment in bringing out the best among both rich and poor, it would be committing a crime against humanity.

As John XXIII reminded us, ". . . in some nations economic life indeed progresses, but . . . not a few men are to be found, who have no concern at all for the just distribution of goods. . . . Accordingly, there are not lacking grave dangers in the help provided by the more affluent nations for development of the poorer ones. For among the citizens of these poorer nations there is operative a general awareness of the higher values on which moral teaching rests—an awareness derived from ancient traditional custom which provides them with motivation.

"Thus, those who seek to undermine in some measure the right instincts of these peoples, assuredly do something immoral. Rather should those instincts be honored, refined and perfected, since upon them true civilization depends."[4]

[4] *Mater et Magistra: Christianity and Social Progress.*

21

The Leaven of Christianity

*It is evident that both the solidarity of the human
race and the sense of brotherhood which
accords with Christian principles, require that
some peoples lend others energetic help in
many ways. Not merely would this result in a
freer movement of goods, of capital, and of men,
but it would also lessen imbalances between
nations.*

—John XXIII

The West must turn even more often towards Christianity,
if it is to revise its scale of values. The Christian nations,
certainly on the sociological level, do not seem to present a
united front. Catholics, Anglicans, Lutherans, and Calvinists
often seem to have a less burning desire to conquer the
world for Christ than that displayed by the many minor
sects in the non-Christian countries and in South America.
Christians everywhere are, nevertheless, concerned with the
moral aspect of economic questions and with the social consequences of the Gospel's message.

An anthology published under the general editorship of
the Reverend A. Dudley Ward seems to provide an adequate

expression of the attitude of the "Federal Council of Churches."* He reacts against the "fanatical cynicism and false philosophy which is in opposition to the very foundations of our Western society," and affirms that "all men should benefit from the minimum conditions necessary for a decent and wholesome life." In order to achieve these conditions:

Economic power should not place private interest above public benefit.

It should not limit opportunities for cultural advancement or for financial success.

It should not suppress freedom of opinion.

It should not dominate the creative dynamism of the economy by any other means.

This book, unfortunately, is not entirely free of American oversimplifications, and it does not draw the conclusions which the universal application of the principles it enunciates makes inevitable.

Generally speaking, the social concepts of Anglo-Saxon Protestantism seem to have been outstripped by French Protestantism, at the heart of which the "Christian Social" movement deserves special mention.

Nonetheless few will be surprised if we choose to consider here the Catholic effort, whose steadfastness from the doctrinal point of view and whose fidelity to the Gospel continue to attract increasing numbers of those whom the Catholic Church lovingly describes as her "separated brethren." The demands made by truth, as witnessed on all sides during the ecumenical meetings of the past few years, and the serious

* *Goals of Economic Life,* ed. by A. Dudley Ward (New York: Harper, 1953).

nature of the work to which these have given rise, show how painfully the division of Christianity is felt. At the same time, they are a pledge that efforts towards unity will be on a level that is divorced from that of political tactics.

Numerically, Catholics cannot muster a force similar to that of the nations involved at Bandung. Before China became Communist, Catholics were outnumbered by the many branches of Buddhism. At the present rate of growth, it is not certain that the increasing Catholic population will continue to account for the same proportion of humanity. While they continue to make conversions, Catholics also sustain many losses.

It is still difficult, despite the considerable amount of recent research into religious sociology, to discover the degree of attachment which Catholics have for their Church. While the research carried out in Italy may dispel some illusions, that undertaken in France shows us that the "eldest daughter of the Church" is much more Christian than is immediately obvious, and all the more so because personal religion has replaced sheep-like obedience.

Unfortunately, Catholics are divided on social problems. While most take to heart the social teaching of the Church, which has been continually expounded by the Popes from Leo XIII to Paul VI, and endeavor to put it into practice, there is a rear guard which is deaf to the appeals of the Catholic hierarchy both where the more equitable division of land and other sources of wealth are concerned, and where the Church's appeals to disseminate the principles of social justice throughout the world are involved. This rear guard believes that the preservation of the established order of things is absolutely necessary, as well as the preservation of its privileges, so that it can be sheltered from new and generous developments and from courageous initiatives.

It is obvious, nevertheless, that the progressives will succeed—despite the excesses in both speech and behavior with which some of them can justly be reproached. "The letter kills and the spirit inspires." Every Catholic country has its Christian élite—and its members are drawn from all social classes—who are steeped in the two fundamental principles of justice: active respect for every man, and the effective propagation of the general well-being. These Catholics acclaimed the Encyclicals of John XXIII and the work of the Vatican Council.

In *Mater et Magistra* John XXIII considers the relationship between economically well-developed communities and countries which are in course of development as "the most important problem of our time." After noting that "today men are so intimately associated in all parts of the world that they feel, as it were, as if they are members of one and the same household," he shows that this lays an obligation on the more fortunate to help those who are "overcome by poverty and hunger," and he stresses the particular duty of Christians:

. . . As can be readily deduced, and as the Church has always seriously warned, it is proper that the duty of helping the poor and unfortunate should especially stir Catholics, since these people too are members of the Mystical Body of Christ.

Pacem in Terris recapitulates and defines the essential themes of *Mater et Magistra* concerning the assistance to be given to developing countries. "It is vitally important, therefore, that the wealthier states, in providing varied forms of assistance to the poorer, should respect the moral values and ethnic characteristics peculiar to each, and also that they should avoid any intention of political domination. . . . If this be done, it will help much toward shaping a community of all nations, wherein each one, aware of its rights and duties, will have regard for the prosperity of all."

The essential role of the Church is not of course an economic one. The Church brings to the human race, to all men of good will, the message of spiritual salvation through adherence to Jesus Christ, the Son of God, who is equal to his Father in the unity of the Trinity, but is also a true man, the son of Mary. The Church's essential task is to bring the glad news of salvation. Fully realized humanism is humanism which is completed by the possession of God and the sight of him face to face.

However much it may be concerned with the divine, the Christian message is also deeply attached to humanity, because it contains the commandment of love: "Love one another as I love you." This is the message of Christ, who loved his own people and all humanity to the point where he died for them.

The Christian message, through this its great commandment of love, has a greater potential for civilization than any other. When any group of people comes to understand this, that group becomes fraternally united. When the people who claim to embody a Christian civilization put it into practice, the world will straighten itself out.

Respect for man, and for every man, an active respect that is not satisfied with abstention from evil, but brings about the establishment of the common good on all levels of human solidarity—this is the reply to mankind's demands for the future.

It can also be said that the Christian message has never before found a world so ready to receive it. As civilizations disintegrate, the Christian nations can snatch a helpless humanity from the jaws of despair by exhibiting a genuine, really incarnate Christianity divorced from every form of greed. This may seem Utopian, and it may well be; but even if it were only partially realized, it would correct the trend of history.

It is surprising that Christian schools, colleges and universities, as well as Catholic Action groups, fail to teach with all the authority at their disposal, the necessary judgments on the relationships between different nations which have always been enshrined in the Church's teaching and which she will never cease to emphasize.

The fact is that Christians, like others, are enmeshed in the deterministic attitudes of their own civilizations. They have always been some distance behind the message, and they will continue to be so. They can however approach closer to it, and anyone who looks at the world today will agree that this is beginning to happen. Authentic Christianity is beginning to flourish everywhere; but, as plants need time before they grow and flourish, this slow development may irritate us by its apparent tardiness and air of compromise.

Christian thinkers are at work in Europe, in the Americas, in Africa, and in every vantage point which they still hold near the countries from which they are being expelled. They are fired by a zeal to recapture the lost years, to integrate every scientific and sociological development into the Christian vision, so that they can provide the world with a new framework of essential knowledge responding to the new demands of the spirit and far surpassing the pragmatic philosophies on which the West has relied, as well as the great dynamic but erroneous plan which Marxism has been unable to operate.

Anyone who follows the advance of Christian thought and the progress of Christian commitment in all the spheres of research and action, can see that a new Christian strength is taking shape in a way which matches up to the demands of the modern age.

Christians everywhere—even though they may be occasionally harassed by their rear guard—are maturing silently and through experience. They are preparing to cope with the inevitable collapse of the inhuman materialistic systems, with myths based on quick profits, and with fables which are incompatible with reason.

While everything seems to give the impression that Communist expansion is becoming more and more probable, it is nevertheless true that Communism will not be able to endure if it does not reject many of its basic doctrines. Enlightened Christians today, on the contrary, can draw fervently on their sacred texts and on their tradition while they direct their efforts, at the same time, towards the total reality of the world as it appears from the scientific point of view. Their narrow conception of economics has ceased. When they re-read the writings of the Fathers of the Church, they will discover in them demands whose significance in the sphere of international relations they have never fully understood. St. Basil's homilies will assume an increased significance and a stirring up-to-dateness in their eyes. They can, by making a simple transposition of names, reproach avaricious groups of people and avaricious countries with the same words as St. Basil used as a reproach to the solitary miser. They can repeat to the rich:

Whom do I wrong in keeping what is mine, you say? Tell me, what is yours? From what source have you received the things which you have used for your own benefit?

This bread that you have, it belongs to the hungry; the coat that you keep in your wardrobe belongs to the naked; the money that you hoard unused belongs to the needy. This is why those you wrong are as numerous as those whom you might have been able to help.

Enlightened Christians can reproach nations which refuse genuine aid to the underprivileged countries with these words, which St. Basil put in the mouths of the privileged men of his own day:

We receive and we give not to others. We praise generosity, but we deprive the poor of it. We are freed slaves, but we do not pity our companions who remain under the yoke. We were hungry, and now have a surfeit of possessions, but we ignore the needy. While we have God as a magnificent patron and provider, we have been stingy towards the poor and refuse to share our goods with them. Our sheep are fruitful, but more numerous are the people who go naked. Our barns are too small to contain all that we possess and yet we do not pity those in anguish.

When Christians have come to a fuller realization of the demands made by their doctrine in the light of mankind's position today, the cries of their consciences will reach even the most hardened governments. If Christians prove themselves to be really committed to the progress of the social and human sciences, if they accept poverty—and they must also suffer, as St. Paul said—and dedicate themselves to their cause even unto death, in imitation of Jesus, they can be the most influential and the most effective members of the human race.

If present tendencies continue, they will probably play a major part in the evolution of a new civilization—if such a civilization is to arise. Their ambition must be universal without attempting to dominate the world. The Christian presence in the world according to the Gospel is "a leaven." Their success depends on the degree of intensity of their service to mankind. Where they are personally concerned, they will achieve their civilizing work courageously and yet modestly by seeking the kingdom of God with intelligence and zeal. As a Christian and a Catholic priest, I cannot analyze the situation of humanity, or the forces which are threatening or reshaping it, without drawing attention to the great hope with which the reawakening of Christianity must inspire us.

Part Seven

Demands Made by a New Civilization:
GENERAL CONCLUSIONS

It is impossible to escape a feeling of alarm after reaching the end of this analysis, which I have tried to make as objective as serious documentation available at present has allowed.

The greatest evil, certainly, is easily distinguished: three-quarters of humanity are either hungry or undernourished; and the undernourished are, for the most part, those who are most prone to the socially destructive diseases other than hunger. The deficiency diseases are accompanied by those carried by parasites and by virus diseases. For the huge majority of those living in urban areas housing is precarious, inadequate and unhealthy; families live almost in one another's laps in conditions of unmitigated promiscuity. The prevalence of this sort of situation is increasing, because poor people cannot prevent the purchase of land near the area where they work. The machinations of landlords and speculators push them even further out into the new outlying areas which no one has thought of designing with a view to the needs of collective living. The administrative, commercial and industrial townships have become giant monsters whose arms encircle an extremely congested town center.

In spite of this, towns—and cities even more so—continue to attract people from rural areas who are trying to escape from their insecure existence. This is because land in the rural areas is frequently subject to erosion, salination, and division among more and more owners; years of drought follow one another, the family home is dislocated, and the diminishing size of the allotments means that the bare minimum can no longer be produced. Farms are seized by money-lenders; they are mechanized, thus reducing the need for farm laborers; or they are turned over from tillage to pasture. If the inhabitants want to continue living, they have to leave, even though for some of them this means death on their journey. Then when they reach the cities, they have to wait for a considerable time, and in a state of complete deprivation, before they can obtain a job that may itself be of uncertain duration.

I am not speaking here as a mere writer, but as a careful observer of social reality in Latin America, Africa, and Asia. He who confines himself to piling up statistics, however terrible, can remain unaffected by the appalling difference between standards of living in different parts of the world, and can discuss theories of growth, investment and development without a touch of anguish. But how many of those who have travelled over the underdeveloped part of the world have not been more moved than if they had stayed at home, content to flip through piles of statistics?

The greatest evil in the world is not the poverty of those who are deprived, but the lack of concern on the part of those who are well off.

The spirit of the deprived masses, however, is awakening as their knowledge increases. The era of passive acceptance on the part of the masses is on the way out. A number of factors including a growth in literacy, the press, the radio, and the blatant ostentation of the dominant cliques in the self-governing countries, as well as that of visiting foreign representatives, all contribute to the growing awareness of the deprived nations that a fraction of mankind has too much of the world's goods. In these circumstances, the masses cannot continue to be resigned. Reaction, under many different forms, is taking the place of passive acceptance everywhere. Resignation is a thing of the past. And this reaction is directed principally against those in the West, because the people in the underdeveloped parts of the world are acutely aware of the commodities and consumer goods which the West reserves to itself, and of their own constant desire to acquire these. The world is continually agitated by the nationalistic struggles of people who are under any form of domination. Colonial territories, too, have experienced this reaction, which has also enlisted in its support independent countries who feel that their autonomy is indirectly threatened not only by economic maneuvering, but by all forms of aid that are less than altruistic.

In this way the developed Western half of the world is being deposed from its position little by little. The unity of the underdeveloped world against the West hardens into reality; and reaction which originally had no definite aim has found in the West a clearly defined target. China, freed from Western influence, can be held up as a progressive "model," with the implication that to imitate her is to ensure rapid prosperity.

The disaster is that the West does not understand the situation and moreover does not seem to want to understand.

It is confined by the precedents of its out-of-date past, whether directly colonialist ideas are involved, or whether it is a question of their adherence to a doctrine and an economic system which has become obsolete in relation to the needs and hopes of the poorer countries.

The West, preoccupied with the task of protecting or increasing the wealth it has already acquired, shows that it is powerless to understand the world crisis. It confines its thinking to defense when it should be considering the betterment of humanity as a whole. Because it is tied to the idea of a narrow, profit-based economy, it does not see the necessity of establishing a universal form of economy based on other people's needs. This is a necessity which its main rival, Communism as it exists today, affirms at least in principle. The West's defense against Communism has become an obsession, while at the same time the West fails to realize that Communism cannot be conquered by force of arms. It can only be conquered by the reconversion of Western economic power and culture to the service of the entire human race. Out of motives of self-interest alone, the West continually thinks of military alliances and strategic bases, when it should be considering the possibility of genuinely fraternal cooperation.

The West can no longer claim to be the creator of civilization at a time when a new, universal civilization is already imminent, whose principles have already been enunciated by the United Nations Declaration of Human Rights. At a time when all efforts should be mobilized to put countries in a position to exercise these rights, the West is haggling about the implementation of scanty aid programs. Help is given because of greed and fear, not in justice or in love; and yet people are surprised that this sort of help is met by hardly any reaction other than scorn, aggressiveness and resentment.

The West is committing suicide by trying to be too careful of its own alleged interests. It does not understand that it cannot continue to exist if it does not become a "West without frontiers."

The problem, basically, is one involving a complete revaluation of a scale of values which will lead to a new conception of world development and to new forms of relationships between different countries, even if they happen to be Communist ones.

The Western world, by leaving the field clear for Communists to pretend that they alone are defending the rights of mankind in an integrated manner, is leaving the world open to the attraction of an illusory form of humanism, while, at the same time, it fails to fulfill its normal task in relation to the countries already dominated by Communism.

The tragedy is that the West, by its actions, has turned its back on the scale of values with which it was endowed by Christianity, and which is today the only scale of values that could inspire a new civilization.

In this scale of values a person is esteemed for himself, for his present and potential value. It cannot therefore countenance slavery, under any pretext whatsoever, but must help each man to become a person who is fully free, emancipated from poverty and rendered capable of choosing, in the light of full knowledge, his life's final destination. The West, which holds itself out as a champion of liberty, still wants to put liberty at the mercy of an economic regime which abuses freedom. Its campaigns for liberty abandon the world to the determinisms of economic machinery, through the medium of which different financial groups violate the basic principles of free enterprise of which they never cease to boast.

Western materialism reduces those who are privileged to the status of profiteers and those who are not to the ranks of the exploited, or of beggars.

The success that the West has achieved, where its own standard of living is concerned, has made the rest of the world hungry for more possessions rather than anxious for the improvement of their own basic condition. The Westerner's opportunities to enjoy surplus goods are increasingly envied by the undernourished masses. At the same time, politicians in the newly independent states, instead of guiding production and trade in such a way as to ensure that the greatest number of people will reach at least subsistence level, open doors which allow the small and favored sections of the population to enjoy even more of the luxury for which they hunger.

The "greedy" civilization has aroused in the great majority of mankind feelings of envy so strong that they must lead to a growing dissatisfaction which will break out suddenly into attempts at revolt.

A civilization of betterment, based on the equitable distribution of possessions, is the only one which should be encouraged. This "betterment" is not only a function of possession. When food is above subsistence level and human dignity is assured, the intense desire to possess even more characterizes a rapacious society.

The laws which have been developed by profiteers to protect their privileges, have given rise to the situation where the promotion of the common good is no longer possible.

The greatest evil is therefore unconcern rather than poverty; it is the unconcern of the technically evolved nations and their governments in the face of a world which will never be the same again. It is also the unconcern of those anxious to undertake development and who, on the basis of poor advice from either East or West, fail to perceive in a clear way and in all their ramifications, the conditions necessary for overall harmonious development.

If the West is to ensure its own survival, it will have to make a radical change in its outlook. It is a matter of urgency that it should agree to play the entire game openly and fairly. What is at stake is the advancement of the whole world, and the rules of the contest are those governing the way in which every country and population group can advance from a less human form of existence to a more human one at the fastest possible rate, at the lowest cost, and taking into account every form of solidarity between different nations.

Complete fairness and openness is necessary if the more suspicious countries are to be convinced that advantage is not being taken of them. Rich countries will have to understand that the day of the small, egotistical alliance is over. The time is rapidly approaching when these countries will be faced with the prospect of losing, not part of what they have, but all that they have. By agreeing to lose a little now, they can put themselves with all the resources at their disposal at the service of humanity. In reality, they will grow in stature if they reply in this way to mankind's passionate appeal for help. They will lose everything if they allow disillusion and hatred to build up in the hearts of the deprived peoples of the world until the latter abandon themselves in despair to internal anarchy or, under dictatorships, to even more serious conflict.

If the West is to survive, not only will it have to make itself loved for the fact that it has learned to love others, but it will also have to show that it is technically capable of helping mankind to overcome material difficulties and to adopt a policy of growth combined with unity.

In spite of the inadequacy of the economic and social sciences, the difficulty is no longer the inability to enumerate the needs and resources of every country and of every people, nor the inability to put into action the necessary measures to remedy the world situation as it is evaluated. If this became the primary aim, it would be possible to ascertain the importance and relative urgency of different forms of development and to plan the stages, as well as appropriating sufficient manpower and means of production to pursue development programs planned by reliable experts and approved by the local governments.

Emergency aid relief measures will have to be made available during the period when these plans are in their infancy or in a transitional stage. There will have to be a great amount of patience shown both by the helpers and the helped. In fact, misunderstandings which have piled up over the years are not all blown away easily; illusory ambitions do not come to terms quickly with hard facts, and not every mistake can be avoided; they will have to be progressively corrected.

The main thing is that it should be made clear that the West has undergone a revolution in that it wants sincerely and intelligently to see the universal good brought about.

The important thing is the conversion to the world-wide view. The West still embodies the germ of this view in the Christian teaching that we must respect every man and strive for attainment of the common good on the basis of unity in all human groups. Universal solidarity has become so obvious today that if the West refuses, through greed or laziness, to come to terms with it in both words and actions, Western civilization will inevitably be destroyed. The forcible techniques to which the West would have recourse in such a situation would only aggravate an incurable disease through the use of power without love.

I hope sincerely that this book, coming after so many other warnings, will stir the conscience of many in the West into wakefulness. I also hope that it will save those people who have already begun their own autonomous development plans from utopian and wishful thinking.

The accomplishment of integrated development on a universal plane is the greatest and most difficult task that mankind has ever had to perform. Left to themselves, the wisest statesmen would be unable to succeed. What is needed over and above knowledge is the collective will of peoples who are moved by clear social forces. And it appears that these forces could be quickly mustered if all men of good will were presented with an objective view of the world crisis and of the threat to mankind.

My sole ambition in writing this book is to encourage and assist this revelation

I would not wish this book—which is an honest attempt to evaluate the situation—to induce in either young or old a feeling of despair or of mere resignation. I do not want the reader to say: "What use is it for us to fight the impossible, and what can we do singly in the face of the destructive forces which surround us? Imprisoned in the Western way of life and hindered by Western economic structures, what can we do? We are also limited by our family and our social obligations. We just haven't the chance, and maybe not even the courage, to go and put ourselves directly at the service of the millions who are hungry, at the service of the universal common good."

It is quite true that there is a great and important need for the numbers of people who are ready and capable of coming to the direct aid of countries in the process of development. The need is great and there are too few workers to meet the demand. At the same time, this is not everyone's job. But there is still plenty to do for those who are not called to this kind of service, or who do not feel that they are technically or morally strong enough to undertake work of this kind.

Poverty and distress are at their own doors, and in their own countries—countries which give scandal every day by purveying counterfeit charity. The West will be an even better example to follow, when it has solved its own problems, when it shows itself more willing to accept in a fraternal spirit the underprivileged workers from abroad who come to work in the developed countries, and when it abandons the golden calf of ever-increasing wealth.

The man who does not leave his own country to help the world, can still help to lay the basis for a new, fraternal humanity and for a race of young people who will later come to give themselves completely to the task. He can do this by assisting all he can to persuade political leaders to adopt a liberal policy towards the underdeveloped countries; by helping to direct the economy towards those who have most need of it, and not to the satisfaction of our own desires; by teaching children to love everyone and above all to love their helpless, wretched neighbors; and by using only the bare necessities for himself in order to assist in the harmonious improvement of the condition of others.

The essential thing is not to lapse into passivity, but to love, over and above the narrow circle in which we live, everyone whom we know to be in any form of trouble.

The solution to the world's problems can be founded only on love, and all genuine love has a universal quality. It is always possible for a man to commit himself—no matter where he may be—in such a way that his commitment contributes to the betterment of all humanity. And every man who commits himself in this way, as a servant of justice, ennobles mankind.